you and your LABRADOR PUPPY
in a nutshell

The essential owners' guide to perfect puppy
parenting – with easy-to-follow steps on how
to choose and care for your new arrival

Carry Aylward

NUTSHELL BOOKS

ISBN: 978-1-9161897-4-4

Front cover design by Nutshell Books
Book design by Nutshell Books
Photography: Cai Cheadle, © AdobeStock,
© Dreamstime, © iStock

Printed by Kindle Direct Publishing

First printed 2019

Nutshell Books
3 Holmlea Road, Goring on Thames
RG8 9EX, United Kingdom
www.nutshell-books.com

To you, the reader, for wanting to be a good Labrador owner, and for the super-special puppy you bring into your heart and home.

And for Tessa, the black Lab who bounded off a sea wall, fell 5m into icy, rock-infested water, survived 100m of pulling tides, and lives – in the flesh and in these pages – to tell the tale.

CONTENTS

FOREWORD

You might have come across a few Dysons and Hoovers lately. A couple of them might even have been vacuum cleaners. As for the rest? They were probably Labradors – devoted followers who slurp up any spillage and lick the floors till they shine; who bark at strangers because they can't WAIT to meet new people, invite them inside and show them around; and whose big love, burly builds and boisterous bounding will literally bowl you over.

But in spite of their insatiable appetites, misguided watchdogging efforts and unbridled affection, the Labrador is, year after year after year, the world's favourite dog breed. It has been the top dog in the US every year since 1990, and the (UK) Kennel Club calls it "The most popular of all pedigree breeds …"

Is this because they are such handsome-looking dogs? Because they have such lovely natures? Because of their devotion to their owners? … Yes, yes and yes. It's all of the above. It's because Labradors really do tick all the boxes. At the risk of sounding boring, they are the universal part, the one-size-fits-all of the dog world. Good all-rounders, they are not too energetic, not too aloof, not too independent, too large, too small or too hairy.

With their big, warm hearts and no trace of aggression, they are everyone's best friend. They get on well with other people, they are good with children, they get on well with other dogs and are generally good with other animals too. Their reputation as 'Labradorable' is well earned, and it's no wonder they are seldom found in rescue centres.

As if that's not enough, Labradors have relatively few health issues (as long as they've been responsibly bred), and they are generally easy to train. They are compatible with a wide range of lifestyles and adapt easily to different geographic environments.

Let's be honest, there are not many dog breeds you can say all that about!

But, whether you already have your Labrador puppy, or you are seriously considering inviting all that Lab love into your life, don't let all this praise for the breed lull you into a false sense of security.

Inviting a dog into your life – even the world's #1 dog – and especially a puppy, is still a hugely daunting venture. But it's a hugely, wonderfully exciting one too. The first few months will be a rollercoaster ride of pure exhilaration and hair-pulling frustration. You will gain love and laughter by the barrel, and you will lose valued possessions and many hours of sleep. There will be flashes of obedience and pure genius from your puppy, and they will be matched with slip-up moments that have your head spinning with horror.

Of course, there's no getting a Labrador into a 'nutshell' – realistically speaking the nutshell is far more likely to be inside the Lab. Besides there's far too much substance between those wet noses and the tips of those table-sweeping tails. What this book does offer in a nutshell is the most up-to-date, practical advice for new, or out-of-practice, owners on choosing and raising a Labrador puppy.

The book flows chronologically, from the decision to invite a Labrador into your life, through finding and choosing your puppy and preparing for the homecoming. It advises you on picking up your puppy, and walks you through the first days, weeks and months – the vital early stages.

The first few months of his life really are the time that shape the dog he will grow into, so this is absolutely when you need to put the most energy into his upbringing and training. This book makes important information quickly and easily accessible, because this stage slips by surprisingly quickly and there are many things you shouldn't wait to find out only once you have the time for more in-depth study.

For the sake of easy reading it uses a concise format with simple-to-follow Dos and Don'ts; the Labrador Retriever is referred to as Labrador or Lab; and your puppy is referred to as 'he', but please consider 'he' to mean 'she or he' in every instance.

These pages are tailored to help you build a solid foundation for a wonderful relationship with your dog. So whether or not you've had a Labrador, or in fact any dog, before now, congratulations on taking this step to being or becoming the best puppy parent you can be.

Let's get started.

1. AREYOU READY?

Labradors aside for a moment, are and your family truly ready for a dog? Any dog? Because in all seriousness being a dog owner is no whirlwind ride at the funfair. It's a momentous, life-changing and long-term decision!

If you are new to owning a dog, you should know that when you invite one into your world, your life will never be the same. You will soon start thinking differently about what you wear, the places you visit, your holiday destinations, the car you drive and, yes, even your next house. Your life will also be warmer, stinkier, happier … richer in so many ways.

If you invite a dog into your home, he should be treated like family. Ask yourself very honestly whether, at this time in your life, and for the next ten to twelve years, you will be able to give him:
- the love,
- the time,
- the money,
- the space,
- the exercise,
- the care,
- the training
- and the patience

he needs and deserves?

Because **no** dog should ever be cast aside like a pair of shoes its owner has grown tired of.

Do you have other pets?

If you have other dogs or cats, consider carefully how a new dog would fit in to your family. If you get your Lab, especially as a puppy, there's no reason for him to be a problem with your other pets. Your other pets, however, might not be quite so adaptable.

Is a puppy right for you?

Ask yourself honestly whether you can face the puppy stage with the pooping, weeing and chewing of everything in sight. An adolescent Lab can be a real handful – right until around three years of age – and needs a huge amount of training and socialising. Ask yourself whether you have the time and energy. If not, you might consider taking on a dog that has finished with toilet training, teething and even adolescence.

It's not unusual for prospective Labrador owners to find a well-trained, high-quality adult that needs rehoming, and this option is one that could save you hours of hard work.

Another option is to contact an established and reputable breeder to find out if you can give an ex-breeding dog the chance to live as a pet. Or you could take on a dog that hasn't performed as well as expected in the show ring. Similarly, some really super Labs that have been selected and trained for work as guide dogs or therapy dogs, simply don't pass all the tests and need family homes instead.

Do you value the quiet life?

Have you considered giving a home to a dog in its senior years? If you can find one, there is little more rewarding than taking on a retired working Labrador. But there are many beautiful older dogs that need re-homing through no fault of their own, so if you are no longer as active as you once were, this might be the best choice for you now.

An older dog is likely to take longer to adjust than a puppy but as long as he has been treated well, a Labrador will love you as his ever-own, no matter how old he is when he becomes yours.

You still want a puppy?

I know. They're warm and cuddly and there's nothing as sweet as the pitter patter of puppy feet. But the first steps to getting a puppy are a big investment – not just financially, but also in terms of time, energy and emotion. This is not an effort to put you off getting a dog. Quite the opposite. It's just really important that you are sure you are able to give your puppy the happy life it deserves and fully understand the commitment you're making. Too many dogs are re-homed and even put down each year because their owners underestimated the responsibility.

In a nutshell

If you're sure you can give your dog the love and attention he needs and deserves; and you're sure a puppy is the way forward; and you're brave enough to let those four extra feet bound freely through your heart-space, then let's look more closely at the specifics of taking on a Labrador.

2. IS A LABRADOR RIGHT FOR YOU?

We've already touched on how popular this breed is and why. Labradors are a good choice for people of all ages, lifestyles and climates, and besides, you're already drawn to the breed or you wouldn't be reading this. But it is still worth asking whether a Labrador is right for you. And, just as importantly, whether you and your circumstances are right for a Labrador. So here are some defining features to help with your decision.

Emotionally

Labs really excel here. They are loving and good-natured, happy and optimistic. Honestly, what more could you want?

Temperament-wise

Well they get top marks here too. They are:
- friendly, sociable and playful
- obedient, cooperative and eager to please
- tolerant, yielding and biddable
- open and trusting
- even-tempered, gentle and kind.

Mentally

They are intelligent and alert.

Physically

Labradors are lovely looking dogs – medium to large, powerfully built, with short, weather-resistant coats and kind, attentive eyes. They are strong and agile, and can work for long hours in difficult conditions.

Versatile

It's no wonder Labradors are commonly considered the ultimate, multi-purpose breed. Blessed with all these qualities, they make outstanding:

- **family pets:** they are loyal, loving, willing and great with children.
- **service dogs in the police and military:** their exceptional sense of smell makes them ideal sniffer dogs for search and rescue operations, and the detection of narcotics and explosives.
- **medical detection dogs:** they are able to detect a range of illnesses including cancers, malaria and diabetes.
- **guide dogs:** their intelligence coupled with their caring natures make them excellent guide dogs for the blind and hearing dogs for the deaf, not to mention therapy dogs for children and the elderly.
- **working dogs:** with their soft mouths, good noses and remarkable retrieving instincts, they make fantastic gun and field dogs and are hugely popular with field sports enthusiasts.
- **show dogs:** obedient and agile, they excel in the show ring too.

So, what's not to love?

These awesome dogs get gold stars all round, so what reasons might you find not to choose one for yourself or your family?

Motivated by food ...

Yes, Labradors have voracious appetites – some more than others, but all of them to some extent. This food obsession is not always a bad thing though. For one, training with treats as a motivator works like a dream. But as a Lab owner you do constantly need to keep food out of reach. And you need to carefully monitor your dog's weight.

... and a variety of non-edibles

It's not always food your Lab will tuck into – these dogs are chewing machines. Foods and non-food items will go down the hatch – socks being a universal favourite. This is worth considering before you invest in your loving Lab, or that expensive new pair of socks.

Not good as guard dogs

While some Labradors could pass as watchdogs, alerting you to strangers or visitors, they are not good as guard dogs. They were bred to retrieve rather than hunt, and they are simply too friendly.

Large

Labs both need and take up a lot of room! This means they are better suited to large houses, and ideally large outdoor areas too.

Heavy

And they are solid, so there's no scooping your Lab up under one arm when you need more control – and certainly not when they're fully grown.

Cost

As with all dogs, the expense is a consideration. After buying your puppy, the cost of pet insurance, vets' bills, food, toys and care is no small consideration.

Weak strains and traits

Labradors are generally healthy as breeds go. They can suffer from joint and eye problems, but you can minimise the risk of either of these by choosing a puppy from a responsibly-bred litter with the relevant health clearance certificates. (See the section: 'Buying responsibly'.)

Shedders

People often think of Labs as dogs that don't need much grooming. And with some Labs, some of the time, this is true. But essentially Labradors are shedders. Some shed all year round and others, more considerately, do their main shedding over just two or three bursts a year. When they are shedding you need to be brushing daily, if not twice daily – and that's just the dog. So if you don't like the idea of hair in your house then think twice before inviting a Labrador into your home.

Water babies

Labradors are swimmers. They love water and there's no getting away from that. They are believed to hail from the Newfoundland dog in Canada, a breed that was used by fishermen to retrieve fallen fish and nets from the water, even in the iciest conditions. Most Labs will grab any opportunity to put their dense, water-repellent coats to the test – even in the filthiest of pools – so it's worth considering how you're likely to respond to your dog's wet and often-muddy bounds of affection.

Need exercise

While Labradors are not dizzyingly hyper-active, they do have a lot of energy and this does need channelling, so a short walk around the block won't do. We're talking two hours' exercise or activity a day here. They love running around, especially off the lead, and through all manner of terrain. If you have an aversion to exercise, or don't have a large property for your dog to roam, then a Labrador – and a Working Lab in particular (see 'Strains of the breed' in Chapter 3) – is not a good choice for you.

Need mental stimulation

Labradors love to learn new things and, just like their energy, their intelligence needs channelling. Attention, mental stimulation and training are essential to keep them happy and well-balanced. If you don't or can't give your dog things to do, trust me, he will find things on his own – things that might involve redecorating the furniture for instance. You need to understand now that if this should happen, it would be down to neglect on your part rather than naughtiness on his.

Bottom line

All Labrador puppies have the potential to be great dogs. But they all have the potential to be problem children too. Kept caged or locked up for long stretches, they will become 'difficult': barking, digging and chewing things. But if you can give your Labrador the love and attention he needs and deserves; if you can keep him active and busy – mentally and physically; and if you can give him playtime, toys and walks, you will have love, devotion and entertainment beyond measure. Watch out though, because those big, floppy paws will make big, warm paw-prints in your heart.

3. WHAT IS A 'GOOD' LABRADOR?

You've decided you can give a dog the time, care, expense and devotion it needs, and that you want a Labrador. I'm thrilled for you. There are wonderful, magical, hilarious, sock-nicking, poo-picking, finger-nipping, chin-licking times ahead. And more love than you could ever imagine.

But don't rush off to see the first litter you come across – even if you want no more from your Lab than good company. Why? Because it's close to impossible to resist the pleading eyes of a puppy that wants to go home with you. Once those eyes have found your heart, they are most likely stuck there for life.

Better to plan ahead. Start doing your research so you can make a wise and informed choice. If it's a pet you're after, you'll be less particular than someone who's looking for a show dog or a dog you might be thinking of using for breeding. The puppies could all grow into lovely dogs, but if you don't want to risk weak strains and traits, it's well worth take the time to track down a breeder whose puppies are a credit to the breed.

Here are some things to understand and consider before you begin your search.

Purebreds
Many puppy farmers and backyard breeders mate their dogs with other breeds, and still advertise them as

Labradors. Although these puppies might grow into lovely dogs, they are unlikely to have the traits of a true Labrador. Again this is up to you, but if you do want a purebred – meaning its parents are of the same breed – it is important that you see the mother and, if it's not possible to meet the father, that you at least see photos or video footage of him.

Pedigrees

If you want a pedigree Labrador – a purebred dog that is also registered with a recognised and reputable club or society such as the Kennel Club – you must choose a puppy from a breeder that has their assurance.

And if you are planning to show your dog or become a registered breeder yourself, you will certainly need to do more research. The section 'Useful Information' at the end of the book has a list of organisations and websites you can refer to.

But what is a 'good' Labrador?

Dogs entered into showing classes are measured against the 'breed standard' – a list of desirable attributes specified for its breed by the Kennel Clubs of the particular country.

The following is a summary of attributes considered desirable in a Labrador. Of course your dog needn't tick all these boxes to be a great dog or even a lovely Labrador, but it's useful and interesting to know what the breed standard expects.

Overall

The Labrador was originally bred to be active and agile, with an excellent nose, a soft mouth, an understanding mind, and a love of swimming – with a coat that would protect it from frequent immersion, even in freezing waters.

Temperament is key

A good Labrador is engaged and friendly. He is intelligent, devoted, eager to please, adaptable and kind, with no trace of aggression or undue shyness.

Physical appearance

- **Expression:** intelligent, alert and kind
- **Build:** strongly built and broad
- **Height:** The biggest difference in breed specification between the (UK) Kennel Club and the American Kennel Club (AKC) is the height. In the UK, the ideal male measures 56-57cm (22-22.5") at the wither (the top of the highest point of the shoulder blade), and the ideal female measures 55-56cm (21.5-22"). In America, the ideal male measures up to 61cm (24"), and the ideal female measures up to 59.7cm (23.5").
- **Head:** broad, noble and chiselled
- **Eyes:** brown or hazel, expressing good temperament, intelligence and alertness
- **Ears:** set far back on the head, and hanging close to the head
- **Nose:** wide with well-developed nostrils. According to the AKC breed standard, the nose should be black on Black or Yellow Labs, and brown on Chocolate Labs.
- **Teeth:** upper teeth closely overlap lower teeth
- **Neck:** strong and powerful, set into long, sloping shoulders
- **Chest:** broad and deep through chest and ribs

- **Back:** back line (topline) is level
- **Forelegs:** perpendicular to the ground and well under the body
- **Loins and hindquarters:** broad and strong
- **Tail:** commonly referred to as the 'otter' tail, it is thick at the base and tapers towards the tip. It is of medium length (not too short but extending past the hock) and covered in a dense coat. (Tails should not curl over the backs, and they should never be docked.)
- **Feet:** strong and compact with well arched toes and well-developed pads
- **Coat:** short, straight and very dense, with a soft weather-resistant undercoat. Ideally without wave or feathering, but a slight wave down the back is permissible.
- **Colour:** Labradors come in Black, Yellow, Chocolate (also known as 'Liver') and even Silver (which is new and highly controversial), but only Black, Yellow and Chocolate are acceptable.

    (Golden Retrievers are 'Golden'. Labs are always referred to as 'Yellow'.)

    Black Labs must be black, but Yellow Labs can range in shade from light cream to red fox, and Chocolate Labs can vary from light to dark chocolate. Individual Yellow Labs can have variations in their shading – on their ears and their backs for example. With all colours, a small white spot is permissible on the chest.

Movement

A good Labrador's action is straight, well-balanced, free and effortless.

Faults

Serious faults:

- deviation in height (from the breed standard)
- deviation in colour
- pink nose
- eye rims without pigment
- docked tails.

Causes for concern:

- being overweight
- legs too short in relation to the length of back and depth of body.

Strains of the breed

There are two types of Labrador, most commonly referred to as the Working Labrador and the Show Labrador, and they differ in both appearance and nature.

- **The Working Labrador (also known as the 'American' or 'Field' Lab)**
  This dog is taller than the Show Lab with a lighter, leaner frame. It is longer in the leg and the neck, narrower in the head and has a longer nose. It also has a lighter coat. A Labrador bred fully from the working lines has a higher physical and mental drive than the Show Lab, which makes it better suited to a working life than one as a family pet. That is, unless you can give it the time and exercise it needs.

- **The Show Labrador (also sometimes referred to as the 'English' or 'Bench' Lab)**
  This strain is chunkier and more powerful in appearance than its Working cousin. It is heavier and wider, with a shorter tail, legs and nose, and a

thicker coat. It is calmer by comparison and more patient.

These days most litters are bred with a mixture of the two bloodlines, which makes an excellent combination, but it's well worth checking the balance of these types before going to see the puppies.

4. FINDING THE LITTER

DECIDE WHAT YOU'RE LOOKING FOR

Before you actually go in search of new litters, you might want to sort out some preferences in your own mind. And, unless you live alone, make sure you involve all members of the household in these decisions. It's very important that everyone has bought into the whole idea from the very start. The more say the family has in choosing your dog, the more likely they will be to actively engage with and care for it, and the less likely they'll be to shirk their dog-walking, poo-picking responsibilities.

First of all, are you're happy with just a pet, or do you have particular expectations of your Labrador: as a show dog, for breeding or as a disability assistant for example? If you do, you will need to do in-depth research into the parents' natures, their abilities and their breeding.

If you are wanting your Lab as a pet, these are some first-stage considerations.

Breed strain

Is it a Show Lab you're after, a Working Lab, or a mixture of the two? (See 'Strains of the breed' in the last chapter.)

Coat colour

Deciding on the colouring of your dog can also narrow your search. If it's important to you for your dog to meet the breed standards then he should be one of the three accepted colours: Black, which is the original colour, Chocolate, or Yellow.

All the colours are shedders, so you can't avoid or minimise shedding by choosing your Lab based on the colour of its coat.

There is also no clear difference in temperament based on colour, although some seasoned owners claim that Chocolate Labs are more quirky in nature and can be more fun, but also more challenging.

Girl or boy?

Honestly, that's up to you. If you're not hoping to use him or her for breeding someday, I don't believe there's much in it, and most Labrador experts agree. Males are slightly larger than females in both height and weight (see 'Physical appearance' in Chapter 3), but beyond that, every dog really is his or her own 'person' and any generalisations are dangerously sweeping. Nevertheless, these are some of them.

Females **can** be more demanding of your affection and attention than males, while also being more independent and more territorial. Males **can** be more affectionate, attentive of their owners and more exuberant. They also tend to be more protective and possessive of their food and toys, and more motivated by food.

Neutering is of course an important consideration here. Un-neutered females will come into heat every six months – which could result in mood swings and aggressiveness towards other females – and there is, of course, the risk of unwanted pregnancy. Un-neutered males can go in search of females, and can lift their legs inside the house to mark their territory. Neutering really is the answer for both sexes and there is more on this in the chapter 'Going forward'.

TIMING

The best time to pick up your puppy

Once you have a clear idea of the sort of puppy you're looking for, the next thing to consider is the best time to bring him into your home and family. Labradors are sociable creatures and don't like being alone, so ideally this should be at the beginning of a stretch when most of the family will be home and able to care for him full-time for most – if not all – of the day. If you are retired this might not be a consideration, but if yours is a working family with school-going children, for example, you should try to pick your puppy up early in the school holidays.

The weather is another consideration. If you live in a country where the summer and winter temperatures are very different, or the wet seasons are extreme, then getting your puppy at the start of a warm or dry season will make for much easier exercising and toilet training.

Luckily most breeders are likely to have taken these factors into consideration, so you will find that the most puppies are available at the start of summer and the long school holidays.

The first step then is to decide the date when it will be most convenient for you to take your puppy home. Good breeders won't let their puppies go to their new homes before they are eight weeks old, so work out eight weeks before your ideal date, and – unless you are already waiting for a specific female to have her puppies – that is when you should start looking out for brand new litters.

Ideally you should visit the litter and meet the puppies around the six-week mark, if not before.

When to start looking

If you're looking for a family pet, your search should take no more than a few months.

However, if you're looking for a dog that is competition- or breeding-quality you can expect to be looking for up to two years before actually bringing your puppy home. It is likely you'll be in contact with a breeder before the litter is born, or even before the mother is mated.

And where

Either way, you can make a start by identifying the best route to finding puppies for sale in your area. This might be a Kennel Club, a publication, a website or several of each. (There is more on this in the next section: 'Buying responsibly'). This browsing stage will give you a sense of what the puppies look like when they are newborn and very young, and also of when puppies are advertised – some people advertise their litters very early, and some only when the puppies are almost ready to go to their new homes.

Advertising channels often feature males available for breeding, and if you see a male you particularly like you could ask the owner to keep you informed of new litters he has fathered.

BUYING RESPONSIBLY

You might know someone who has Labrador puppies ready for their forever homes, and they might be the nicest people on earth, but that doesn't necessarily make them good or responsible breeders. Labrador breeders range from excellent, to acceptable, to people who shouldn't be allowed to keep them, never mind use them for breeding. But whether you're turning to friends, word-of-mouth or advertisements (online, in magazines or in newspapers), when you start looking for your puppy, you need to be super-cautious.

You want to be sure you are buying a healthy, happy puppy and, at the same time, not unknowingly supporting the cruel puppy trade. So before arranging to see any litter, always make sure it's with a responsible and reputable breeder whose dogs are health tested, and who have the certificates to prove it.

Good places to look for reputable breeders:

- the websites of the Kennel Club and Labrador clubs in your country

    Breeders approved by the American Kennel Club (AKC) or assured by the (UK) Kennel Club, for example, agree to certain welfare standards, to produce puppies in line with the breed standards, and also to reduce or eradicate genetic illnesses, usually joint and eye problems.

- dog shows.

Good people to ask:

- members of Labrador clubs
- breeders at dog shows
- dog trainers
- dog behaviour experts
- vets
- groomers
- boarding kennels personnel.

Reading the adverts

If you're turning to adverts, make sure you're reading between the lines. Don't look for a bargain – good Labradors usually aren't cheap. And be just as wary of puppies priced well over the average, as silly money is unlikely to guarantee you a miracle dog. But most importantly of all, watch out for puppy dealers.

Dodging the dealers

Also referred to as puppy farmers, these are people who breed puppies in awful conditions, then sell them from normal-looking homes which are, in reality, nothing more than a shop front. Puppy farmers and dealers can be tricky to identify, but these are some telltale signs that should make you think twice about an advert.

- Puppy farmers often use the same contact number on more than one advert. If the advert is posted on the internet, do a search on the number to see if it has been used on any other puppy adverts.
- They often use the same descriptions, word-for-word, in more than one advert. You can search, using a key phrase in the wording, to check for duplicate adverts.
- Photos of the puppies or the parents may also have been used on other adverts. Right click on the photo, then select 'search Google for image' to find out.
- A vet will not vaccinate a puppy before four weeks of age so if a person is advertising a vaccinated puppy that is three weeks old, stay away.
- Don't be fooled by promises of 'free puppy packs'. These don't make the sellers any more legitimate.
- If the breeder claims to be Kennel Club registered, check this with the Kennel Club.
- An inexperienced breeder might use the word 'thoroughbred' instead of 'purebred'.

Making the call

When you're happy with the details given, it's time to make contact. You could do this by email to start with, and many people are more comfortable with email, but you will learn so much more by speaking to the breeder in person. These are some key questions to ask:

- Are you registered with the Kennel Club in your country, or a member of a Labrador breed club?
  - *Not all breeders are, but this is a good place to start. If they say they are, be sure to double check.*

- Did you breed the puppies yourself?
  - *It's imperative that they did for many reasons, one being that you can meet the mother.*
- Is it only Labradors that you breed?
  - *Ideally, this should be 'yes'. Multi-breed breeders are often backyard breeders or puppy farmers.*
- Are the puppies currently in the place where they were bred?
  - *This should be a 'yes' and that is where you need to see the litter.*
- How many puppies are, or were there, in the litter?
  - *It's always best to see the puppies together. Avoid seeing just one.*
- Will I be able to see the puppies' and parents' registration and pedigree certificates?
  - *Ideally 'yes'.*
- Have the parents both been health screened?
  - *It's important to know whether there are any hereditary health problems that might be passed on to the puppies. At the minimum, both parents should have been screened for hips and eyes. There is more on this in the next section, 'The paperwork'. If the breeder doesn't believe in health testing, stay away.*
- What health guarantees are you offering in terms of genetic illnesses?
  - *Because some health issues can be well documented, many breeders supply a guarantee with their pups that covers them against these problems. This will vary from breeder to breeder and the length of the guarantee will range from 12 weeks to a lifetime. A*

good breeder will give you some form of guarantee, and it will be written into the sales contract.

- Are you happy to send me copies of the paperwork?
  - *You could ask to see copies of the more important documents before visiting the litter.*
- How old is the mother? And is this her first litter?
  - *You really want to find out how many litters she has had because a Labrador bitch should have no more than three to four litters in her lifetime. These should never be before she has reached two years of age, or after the age of seven, and litters should be no closer*

together than one a year. A breeder who doesn't respect this is putting money above the wellbeing of the dog and should not be supported or encouraged.

- What will happen to the mother when you've finished breeding with her?
  - *Ideally she will stay part of an already loving home.*
- Can I contact someone who already has one of your puppies for a reference?
  - *As long as this is not the breeder's first litter, they should be able to provide a contact.*
- Are the puppies in good health?
  - *Apart from being in general good health at the moment, you want to check whether they've had any health problems to date.*
- Have the puppies been treated for worms?
  - *They puppies should have received at least one deworming treatment from the breeder before they go to their new homes.*
- Have they been given their first vaccinations?
  - *Vaccination requirements vary from country to country, but initial vaccinations generally comprise two doses with an interval of two to four weeks. The first of these is usually given between four and eight weeks of age.*
- Have they been microchipped?
  - *This is a tiny chip injected under your puppy's skin at the back of his neck. It holds his unique number which links to your contact details and, unlike a collar and tag, it stays there for life. If they have been microchipped that's a bonus, but it's not essential. See 'Visit the vet' in the chapter 'The first week'.*

A good and responsible breeder:

- will be happy to answer all your questions.
- will ask questions of you too, to make sure their puppies are going to excellent homes.
- will be able to compare the parent dogs to the Labrador breed standard.
  If they don't know about the standard, or belittle it, you should stay away.
- will have photos and possibly video clips of the puppies' parents and relatives, and be happy to send you more by phone or email if you feel you need them (especially if a visit means a lengthy journey on your part).
- will keep the puppies in the home with the family, and not in kennels or outbuildings.
- will give you the impression of actively loving and nurturing each pup, as well as the mother, to make sure they are well socialised.
- will be happy to arrange a time for you to visit the puppies and their mother in the place where they were born and raised.
- will be happy for you to have more than one visit before pick-up if you feel you need it.
- might give you references of people who've bought puppies from them in the past.
- might offer to take the dog back if you can't keep it. Some breeders even include a contract requiring you to contact them first if you should ever need to give it up.

A responsible breeder will NEVER:

- offer to deliver the puppy to you.
- offer to meet you at a random place.

- tell you the mother is out at the vets, or for any other reason. If she isn't there, the puppy most likely wasn't bred there, or there could be a problem with the mother.
- suggest that you breed your puppy for money. (Good breeders breed Labradors for the love of Labradors, and seldom make money from their efforts.)
- push you for payment.

Never get a puppy if you have
any doubts about the seller or breeder

Once you've found a litter of puppies you like the look and sound of, and you're as sure as you can be that they're healthy, happy and from a good home environment, set up your visit or visits. Then the countdown begins ...

The comfy blanket

While you're waiting for the day of the visit, find or buy a soft, comfortable blanket or cloth to take with you. This is so that, if you do reserve a puppy, you can leave it with him until you pick him up. It will absorb the smells of mum and the litter mates until then, and help to make the separation less stressful when you take him home with it.

Let this comfy blanket absorb the smells of you, your house and your family before you go. Put it in the dirty laundry basket for a few hours. That should do the trick!

THE PAPERWORK

There's also the inevitable paperwork to follow up on.

All paperwork can be subject to faking; nothing, even in writing, can guarantee how your dog will turn out; and anyway there's no reason your Labrador shouldn't be a wonderful companion without any paperwork at all. But checking the paperwork is an excellent way to minimise the risk.

If the breeder has agreed to send you copies of some or all of the documents, you'll need to check these before the first visit. Aim to see as much in advance as you can. The following is a basic list of what the breeder needs to have shown you or given you **before** you take your puppy home.

Registration papers (where applicable)

These are the certificates that record your dog's registration number. They also serve as proof of his pure ancestry, because to be registered with a legitimate registry, your dog must first have a pedigree. Ideally your dog's registration documents have been issued by a reputable registry like your national Kennel Club, but beware of smaller, lesser-known registries which sometimes register dogs without proof of pure breeding.

Pedigree documents (where applicable)

These show your dog's family tree and list the breeding decisions that have been made. Pedigree papers are less official than the registration papers because a dog that is registered is always a pedigree, but a pedigree dog is not necessarily registered.

Health certifications and ratings

Even if you don't plan on breeding or competing, it's important to check the health clearance certificates and ratings for BOTH parents. At the minimum, they should have been screened for hips, elbows and eyes, and you want to see:

- The hip evaluation or hip score
  Scores range from 0-106, and the lower the better. As a guide 0-4 is excellent; 5-10 is good; over 25 is unacceptable.
- The elbow evaluation or elbow score
  Scores range from 0-3, and the lower the better. Ideally this should be 0 or 1.
- A recent eye certificate
  This should be less than 12 months old and show that the dog is free of eye diseases.
- The eye test results
  OptiGen prcd-PRA. Results should be 'Clear'.

Health guarantees

If the breeder has promised a guarantee against joint and eye problems, or any other genetic illnesses, you should get confirmation of this at your first visit.

Proof of achievements

If the breeder has spoken of any competition achievements by the litter's parents and/or relatives, ask to see proof of this too.

Vaccination and deworming records

You will need this paperwork to take to your own vet, as well as to any training classes your puppy might attend or kennels he might need to board at.

Microchipping details

If the puppies have been microchipped, you will need your puppy's individual number and the name of the provider so you can change the existing contact details to your own.

Sales contract

You could also ask to see the outline of the sales contract to be signed by both parties on pick-up.

5. TIME TO CHOOSE

When the day arrives you'll be eager to get going, but before you set off, remember to take that soft, comfy blanket – ideally smelling of your house and family – to leave with the puppies in case you do decide to take one of them.

WHICH PUPPY?

You will be itching to spend time with the puppies, I know, but don't forget to do these basic checks first.

The owner/breeder

Look for signs of that the puppies are being raised where you are seeing them. You want to be as sure as you can be that this is where they've grown up. If you suspect it is somewhere out of sight then you need to be super cautious.

Try to make sense of the puppies' environment. Is it warm, friendly and homely? Are they being brought up in the house? Are they in clean conditions?

Watch how the breeder interacts with the puppies too. Ideally they are being bought up right underfoot and getting lots of human contact. Puppies that haven't had enough positive human interaction from six weeks of age until the time they go to their new homes can have personality issues for the rest of their lives. This time is out of your hands, so don't underestimate the importance of this check.

The mother

First things first, is she the actual mother? (Sadly this does need checking!) Does she look as though she's just had the litter? And does she interact with the puppies? Do the puppies' colours match with the mating of the sire and the dam? Sometimes you can't tell with Labs because if both parents are Black for example, any of the three colours is possible. However, if both parents are Yellow Labs, the pups will all be Yellow. And if both parents are Chocolate, the pups can only be Chocolate or Yellow.

Once you're confident that this is the mother of the litter, it's well worth spending some time with her, and any other relatives too if possible, to get an idea of temperament. They **must** be friendly and good-natured if that is what you hope for in your puppy. It's also important that they are confident, and not shy.

Another question is health. Do they seem healthy and happy?

The paperwork

Whatever documents you were promised before the visit, ask to see them now. And if you might be interested in showing or breeding going forward, you will need to scrutinise them for anything that could bar your dog from conformation classes, or prohibit his or her progeny from being registered.

The puppies

Finally! With some dog breeds, every puppy in a litter is distinctly different from the next, but with a litter of Labradors pups – especially if they are all the same colour – you will most likely be overwhelmed by a writhing bundle of velvety, heart-melting cuddliness.

So what now?

You've met the mother and possibly the father too, and hopefully seen pictures of other relatives. Looks-wise that is the best indicator of how the puppies will turn out, and presumably you're already happy with that. But don't let down your instantly-falling-in-love guard. Not yet. Not entirely. First study their temperaments and make sure they are:

- happy,
- confident, friendly and interactive,
- interested in you and everything around them,
- energetic.

And make sure they look healthy?

- They should appear well-fed, with no ribs showing, but no pot-bellies either.
- Their noses should be clean, cool and damp.

- Their eyes should be clear and bright, with no tear-staining or discharge. If a puppy blinks a lot, this could be the sign of a problem.
- The ears should be clean and you can test hearing by making a noise behind the puppy to check its response.
- Gums should be pale pink.
- There should be no irritation around the genitals or bottom, or signs of diarrhoea.
- The coat should be clean and soft, with no signs of missing hair, or fleas or ticks.
- Movement should appear free and comfortable.

Which puppy?

All going well, you will be itching to take your pick. But which one? They will be as individual as people, so there are no right or wrong puppies, just ones that are more or less suited to you, your family, your lifestyle and your other pets.

Here are some tips that could help you with your decision:

- If you are absolutely sure you want a girl, you could ask the breeder to remove the boys while you meet the girls, or vice versa.
- Don't rush this. Sit down with the puppies and spend all the time you need with them. Play with them and watch them at play.
- See how they interact with you. If you play with one then turn away, does he follow you? If not, that is a sign that he is more independent than a puppy that does.
- See how they interact with their litter mates. Do they dominate? Do they walk away? Do they play

nicely? This could be an indication of how easy they will be to socialise.

- Study their energy levels. Some will be more active than others and dogs with high energy levels need more exercise.
- Sort out which ones are more submissive, and which more dominant. If you already have a dominant dog, a submissive puppy would be a sensible choice.
- Tell the breeder about your family make-up and circumstances and ask them for their opinion, because they will have experience with the breed and will also have had time to get to know the individual pups.
- As a test, try placing the puppies, in turn, on their backs and gently resting your hands on their chests. The puppies that struggle to get free are less patient than the ones that make little effort to get

away. You can also do this test by gently lifting the puppies off the floor, just a foot or two and for a few seconds, keeping them horizontal.

- You could also throw something for them to see if they run after it, or bring it back.
- If you clap behind them, do they flinch? That might be the sign of a nervous disposition, or an indication of poor hearing.

It's often said that you don't choose your dog or puppy, it chooses you, and many people vouch for this. One puppy might spend your entire visit convincing you he's the one you want to take home.

Whichever pup you choose, when you've settled on your choice, that will be the best dog in the world, and time after time you will ask yourself how you got so lucky.

Before you leave

Money

Assuming you're coming back for the puppy at a later date, the breeder will most likely ask for a deposit to secure your puppy. Make sure that you get a receipt and a written agreement that the contract is only binding if the puppy is in good health when you collect it.

If there is no litter registration number as yet, the breeder should give you a signed bill of sale that includes reassurance that it will be available by the time of sale, along with the registered names and numbers of the puppy's parents.

Puppy contract

Confirm with the breeder that they will have an official puppy contract ready at the time of collection. This should include a health guarantee for the agreed specified period; details of health screening (for the pup and its parents); details of the parents; all information to date on vaccinations, worming, micro-chipping and veterinary visits; and information on the extent to which the pup has been socialised and toilet trained.

Food and care
Find out whatever you can about meals. What are the puppies being fed at the moment? How much and how often? Ask to see the food so you can be sure of giving him exactly what he is used to when you bring him home.

Finally, assuming you're coming back for the puppy at a later date, ask the breeder if you can leave your soft blanket with the litter so that when you pick him up, you will be able to bring all those familiar mummy-puppy smells with him into his new home.

6. PREPARING FOR THE BIG DAY

It almost goes without saying that when you pick up your bundle of joy, and destruction too, you will need buckets of love, oodles of patience and a fantastic sense of humour. But you will also need to do a surprising amount of planning, puppy-proofing and purchasing of paraphernalia beforehand ...

Things to do

- Arrange a date to pick up your puppy. Eight to nine weeks old is an acceptable age, but don't pick him up before he is eight weeks. If you are travelling by car, it should be a day when at least one other person can accompany the driver.
- Book a visit to the vet for about two days after pick up.
- If you have other dogs, make sure their vaccinations are up to date.
- If you will be taking out pet insurance, do your homework now so you can have it in place as soon as you bring your puppy home.
- Puppy proof your home:
  - Secure the property. This is the most important thing you can do to keep your dog safe. If you have a garden or yard, ensure the borders are escape proof.
  - If there is a pool, pond or any deep or dangerous water he could fall into, fence it off.

- Check that there are no chemicals within reach (pesticides, weedkillers, fertilisers, etc).
- Cover or hide electricity cables and wires.
- Secure any unstable furniture such as book cases that could come crashing down.
- Remove sharp objects and small things he could choke on.
- Be aware of any plants in your house and garden that may be poisonous. It's worth checking online for a comprehensive list, but these are some of the more common varieties: Aloe Vera, Asparagus Fern, Azalea, Castor Bean, Corn Cockle, Crocus, Cyclamen, Daffodil, Holly Berry, Foxglove, Foxtail, Ivy (Hedera Helix), Jade (Crassula Ovata), Jerusalem Cherry, Jessamine, Hyacinth, Lily of the Valley, Milkweed, Mistletoe, Nandina, Oleander, Philodendron, Potato, Rhododendron, Sago Palm (ornamental house plant), Tomato, Tulip, Water Hemlock.
- Remove valuables from the floor.
- Apply citronella or anti-chew to everything of great value that will be within his reach.
- Decide on his special place, a suitable comfy space that he can make his own. This is where his crate will be positioned if you choose to use one, or simply his basket and toys. Either way this special place should be somewhere central – somewhere that he can feel safe, but without feeling isolated or excluded. An ideal position would be against a wall in the room that most of you spend the most time in during the day.

Things to buy, make or borrow

- **Soft blanket** – you might already have left this with the litter when you chose your puppy, but if not you'll need one now.

- **A crate (also commonly referred to as a cage, den or puppy pen)** – this is optional of course, but it would serve as your puppy's own space, a special place where he can be safe, quiet and keep his toys. There is more about this in the next three chapters, but for now choose one that is at least big enough for your puppy's basket or bed, toys and bowls – and for a full-grown Labrador to stand up, turn around and lie down in. Wire cages are better ventilated than plastic ones, offer better views, and are easily collapsible for storage or transport.

- **Comfortable bed** – this could be a basket or a dog cushion, the mattress from a baby crib or even a folded blanket, as long as it is soft, comfortable and easily washable.

- **A collar** – choose one that is soft, lightweight and comfortable. He will soon outgrow it and you can choose a sturdier one then if that's what you prefer.

- **A dog tag** – no need for cow bells. Choose one that is small and light and have it engraved with his name and your contact details.

- **A harness** – harnesses offer little control over an adult Labrador but it's a good idea to have one of these for your puppy because they put no pressure on his throat when he is learning to walk on the lead. This should be a suitable size, adjustable, and comfortable.

- **Short lead (up to six feet long)** – again, nice and light. He's only little.

- **Extendable lead** – these can be dangerous and are not always permitted in parks and conservation areas. That said, used carefully and only once your puppy is used to the short lead, an extendable lead can make walks more enjoyable for you and your puppy.

- **Bowls** – go for a non-tip, non-slip design. Also consider a non-spill travel bowl for car trips, and a crate bowl that clips onto the door or side of your puppy's crate so that it can't be overturned. Remember your puppy will be a large dog before long, so consider whether to invest in big bowls, or get small bowls for now and upsize in time.

- **Food** – start with the food your puppy has been given at his breeders. After that you can move him on to the food of your choice. If you are concerned about making the best decision, consult your vet at his first check-up.

- **Treats** – you will need lots of these. They are fantastic motivators when your puppy is first learning the rules, and excellent for reinforcing good behaviour. Choose treats that are suitable for puppies and avoid too many additives and preservatives, including sugar and salt. As a rule of thumb, the fewer ingredients the better.

- **A treat pouch** – a handy pocket for loose treats that keeps your own pockets from constantly smelling of dog food.

- **Chews** – your puppy will spend around four hours of each day munching on things, so it's up to you to provide what you want him to do his chewing on. Chews make a fabulous alternative to table legs and leather shoes, but with a young puppy avoid any chews that can splinter. Antler horns are good, and so are Kong toys filled with treats.

- **Toys** – he will need plenty of toys in all shapes, sizes, textures, colours and smells. He will chew on them, play with them and even snuggle up with them for hours. It's quite possible that he'll favour an old sock over an expensive toy, but can a puppy have too many toys? I think not. (It's wise to avoid giving him old shoes because, smart as he is, he's unlikely to differentiate between old and new when he slips inside your shoe closet.)

- **Anti-chew or citronella** – it's worth investing in either of these to spray onto those things he absolutely must not chew on. Expensive chair legs for example.
- **Poo(p) bags** – choose biodegradable ones to do your bit for the environment.
- **Wee mats/newspaper** – for housetraining
- **Carpet cleaner** – pet friendly
- **Odour eliminator** – pet friendly
- **Hot water bottle** – strong and covered
- **Grooming kit** – brush or glove suited to his coat type, and a dog shampoo
- **Dog seatbelt, pet carrier or dog guard** – if he is likely to travel by car.

Indoor extras

- **Baby gates/stair gates** – these are far better than closed doors for keeping a room off-limits. But stay away from stretch gates that he could get his head stuck in.
- **Exercise/play pen** – this is useful if you are leaving him for a couple of hours because it is big enough (usually about four feet by four feet) for him to sleep, play and poop in if necessary. This can also be an alternative to a crate.

Outdoor extras

- **Kennel** – if your puppy is likely to spend a lot of time outside when he is older, you should consider building or buying a doghouse. There's a vast range of luxury kennels on the market for you to choose from or replicate, but make sure the floor is raised.

Other useful features are:

- a removable side for cleaning (often the floor or door)
- a doorway that keeps wind and rain out of the sleeping area. This could be a hanging rubber dog-flap, a patio space or overhang, or even a double doorway.
- kennel bedding – any kennel will need its own soft bedding.
- **Outdoor water bowl** – large and tip-proof
- **Paddling pool** – if you live in a warm climate or have hot summers, a children's paddling pool is great fun and a fabulous cooler.

Setting the rules

Before you bring your newest family member into your home, it's essential for you and the other existing members of the household to have a serious chat about the rules. Decide among yourselves where your puppy will be allowed, and when. Make sure you are all in agreement about which rooms and pieces of furniture are off-limit. And make sure everyone understands that sneaking the puppy into an off-limit area, or letting it break the rules in any other way, would only be unfair on the puppy in the long run.

Most families will agree that he is not to be allowed on your best furniture, which is sensible, but it doesn't mean you need to treat him like an underling. You can compromise by making sure he has a place he can call his own – a special bed placed next to the forbidden chair for example.

Choosing a name

You could choose this once your puppy is home, but either way his name is more important than you might think. You will be using his name several times a day for years to come so it must be something he will easily recognise.

- Animals respond better to shorter names – one-syllable names with a hard consonant or consonants like Duke or Zac for example, or two-syllable names such as Pop-py, and yes, Dy-son or Hoo-ver. You might love the name Penelope or Ophelia, but your dogs would thank you for calling them Pen or Oophy instead.

- Make sure the name you choose doesn't sound too much like a commonly-used command: No, Sit, Down, Stay, Come, Here, Good or Fetch. Beau and Jo, for example, sound too much like No.

- And don't choose a name that sounds like that of another member of the household. If your mother is called Anne, don't call puppy Dan; if your cat is Tigger, don't call puppy Digger or Trigger.

- Choose a name that is easy to call out. 'M' and 'n' sounds are soft which makes them more difficult to call out loud than harder consonants like 'p', 't' and 'z'. Molly, say, is a less effective pet name than Pippy.

- Never give any dog a name you wouldn't be happy calling out loud in public.

7. PICKING UP YOUR PUPPY

The big day has finally arrived. If possible, pick him up early in the day so he can spend lots of time in his new environment before facing his first night without his mother and litter mates.

Remember, if you are driving, to make sure someone is with you to comfort and hold him.

Before you go

- If you haven't already set up his special place in a safe but central spot, do that now. Crate or no crate, furnish it with the comfortable dog basket or bed, some toys, and also some treats if you like.
- And if you haven't already sprayed your most valued furniture with anti-chew, now's a very good time.

Things to take

- The remainder of the payment (if necessary)
- An absorbent mat (or similar protection) in case he relieves himself in the car
- Poo(p) bags and cleaning cloths
- Two bowls (one for food and one for water)
- A small amount of food (in a container)
- A bottle of water
- A small selection of toys and chews
- A backup soft blanket or cushion is also a good

idea (in case something has happened to the one you left with the breeder)

- A collar or harness and your lead (not extendable).

The big moment

There at last and this is it! Give your new family member and best friend a gargantuan cuddle, have a play and check that he's still in good health:

- happy, confident and curious,
- that there are no signs of mucus from the nose, bottom or genitals,
- and that his ears are clean and not smelly.

'Happiness is a warm puppy'

Charles M Schulz

In the excitement

Apart from your new and perfect puppy, don't forget to come away with:

- the blanket you left, if you left one
- the registration papers
- any other relevant paperwork including:
  - a receipt of payment,
  - vaccination certificate,
  - microchip number and provider details (so you can register your puppy under your name and with its new address and contact details).

It's also worth double checking his food type (just in case it's changed), and be sure to find out what times he has been having his meals.

And last but definitely not least, remember to thank the mother as well as the breeder for your beautiful puppy.

Travelling

Make sure your puppy is feeling safe and happy to be with you before you take him away for good. He is totally reliant on you now, so put yourself into those little paws that are being taken away from their mother and litter mates. Realise that he is leaving the only place he has ever known and, if you're driving, getting into a car for the first time too! Ask yourself, "How would I be feeling now?" and "What would I need from this new person or family?" You'd want to feel safe and secure, loved and cherished.

It's advisable to put on his collar or harness before you set off. This is best done with two people so one of you can hold and distract him while the other puts it on. If you're using a collar, you don't want it too tight or too loose. You should just be able to put two fingers between the collar and the puppy's neck. If you've brought a harness, you should also be able to fit two fingers (and no more) between your puppy and the harness at any point.

If you're travelling by car, the puppy would be happiest being held by the passenger in the back seat. He would need to be held securely, so that the driver is not distracted, and be given love and constant reassurance on the journey. However, where you put him in the car will depend on the laws in your country, as holding him in the back seat could affect your insurance.

Your puppy will probably be too anxious for toys, but offer them anyway.

If the journey home is a long one, you'll need to attach the lead to his collar and stop every hour – more if you can. Like people, dogs can suffer from travel sickness, so it is possible he might be feeling a little ill or even be sick on the journey. He will also need these breaks for a walk and the chance to go to the toilet, but always keep him on the lead. Though he's unlikely to stray from you, this would be a terrible place for him to get loose.

At every break, offer him some of the food and water in the bowls you've brought along.

8. THE HOMECOMING

Give him a chance to wee before going inside.

Carry him into the house and put him near or in his special place, or his crate, with the door wide open. Sit beside him, and if you have a blanket smelling of his mother and litter mates, arrange it in his basket and give him a treat.

Then let him explore his special place and the house, always staying by his side. Let him venture into all the areas he will be allowed to roam, so that he knows this is home. If there are areas of the house that will be off limits to him, then it is better not to let him in there from the start than to change the rules at some later stage.

Even if you intend your puppy to be an outdoors dog, he should have access to at least one room at this stage, because he is not yet ready to be left outside on his own.

All the treats today should be given in his crate or special area to encourage the idea that this is his very own bedroom. His comfy blanket should stay there and it is advisable to feed him there too. Do everything you can think of to make him feel that this is the best and safest place in the world. If there is a crate and the design is very open, cover it with a blanket leaving gaps he can see out of.

Puppies wee about once an hour and poop several times a day, so take him outside every hour if you can. He will still piddle and poop in the house because he is so little, can't talk to you, and most likely has no idea that doing this inside is a no-no. Toilet training is covered in more detail later on, but for now be sure to clean up after him very well, and use an odour eliminator.

Your puppy needs 18-22 hours' sleep a day at this age, and today he is likely to need even more than that. But your presence is essential for his peace of mind so, when you're sitting quietly, let him sit with you and sleep on your lap or close by.

Make sure there is always fresh water available to him, and that he knows where it is. Feed him what he is used to and, as far as practical, at the times he is used to. At this age he is most probably on three or four evenly-spaced meals a day. Aim to give him his last meal of the day a good two hours before his bedtime, so he has a chance to go to the toilet before settling down for his first night.

9. THE FIRST NIGHT

Crunch time! He's had his supper, a couple of hours ago, and it's time for bed.

Take him outside for a last chance to go to the toilet. Stay with him in the place you'd most like him to go, and, be patient. If he goes where you want him to, make a big fuss of him.

Back inside, make sure his crate or safe space is as appealing as possible, with his comfortable bed and his soft blanket. (In the short term, some people make this space in their own bedrooms, setting it up by the side of their beds. Considering the trauma of this first night, to your puppy and yourselves, there is a lot to be said for this. He still wouldn't be able to snuggle up the way he's used to, but at least he could see you and hear you and know he's not alone.)

If his sleeping place is a metal crate, the openness still leaves your puppy quite exposed. So if you've chosen the crate option and haven't already done so, put a blanket over all or part of it, making sure he can always see out.

It's a good idea to make a warm, but not too warm, hot water bottle, and wrap it carefully into his comfy blanket. This is to replicate the body warmth of his mother and litter mates when they're snuggled up. Some people also put a ticking clock in the bed to mimic a heartbeat. And if the special place is not in your room, you could leave a radio playing softly to give him the sense he is not alone.

Scatter some toys and treats and make sure he has access to some clean water in his non-tip or clip-on bowl.

If the space is big enough for a place to relieve himself – aside from the bedding and bowls, then cover this with newspaper or an absorbent wee mat.

When crunch time comes, don't fuss over him. Just put him in his crate or special place with a treat, as though he's the luckiest puppy in the world, and close the door: be it a cage door, room door or baby gate.

In all likelihood he will cry at first, but he'll be warm, comfortable, fed and tired, so it shouldn't be for long.

Don't give him attention when he cries, because then he'll just keep on crying. If you do want to tell him he's a good dog, then wait until he's settled.

What about toilet time? If he is in your room, and you hear him shuffling around in the night, get up and take him outside. He won't want to wee in his crate or sleeping place if he can help it. (And it won't be long before he doesn't need this break at all.)

If he's not in your room, you'll need to set an alarm for the middle of the night so you can get up and take him outside. Alternatively, and only if you've laid down a wee mat, you could wait until very early the next morning. You'll need to repeat this routine for the next few weeks at least.

10. NEW PUPPY SAFETY

People

The best way to keep your puppy safe is through your and your family's and housemates' diligence.

- Be careful to keep doors closed or open, where necessary, and don't shut them too quickly – your new 'shadow' could be right on your heels.
- Don't let your puppy play around cars or tackle the lawn mower.
- Don't leave dangerous objects or poisonous substances in his reach.
- Don't feed him or let him get hold of 'people food', and especially not chocolate!
- Don't let him near the edges of deep water, or high places: balconies, low window ledges, or unsecured staircases.
- Be careful with rocking or reclining chairs.
- Keep electrical cords well out of reach – apart from shock there is the danger of something falling on him (a heavy iron or boiling kettle for example).

If you want to be really proactive, put yourself in his paws for a moment. Being super careful not to underestimate his strength, speed or intelligence, get down on all fours and see what temptations call. Then take these away. Puppy-proof your home and make it as difficult as you can for him to get into any form of trouble.

Then watch over him, just as you would a busy toddler.

Small children

If you have small children, it is very important to supervise them when they are playing with your puppy. There is more on the subject later in the book, when your puppy will have become more boisterous, but small children must understand NOW that your puppy is NOT a toy.

- They must not be allowed to pick him up without adult supervision.
- They must not be allowed to disturb him if he is sleeping or has taken himself to a quiet place.
- They must not run around squealing, and if the puppy becomes over-excited they must calm down and keep still.
- They should be allowed to play calm games with him, but nothing involving wrestling or tugging.
- They should always stay on their feet while playing with the puppy. If children writhe on the ground with your puppy, he will treat them like his litter mates and mouth and bite.

Your other dogs (if you have them)

- Keep introductions short and sweet to start with, with your puppy on a lead to stop him from getting too close.
- If possible, let them meet for the first time away from home. Ideally, choose somewhere your older dog has not been before so that the excitement of the new environment will dilute the puppy's presence. Try to ensure the meeting place is somewhere no other dogs are likely to go (as your

puppy will not be not protected by his vaccinations yet).

- Stand still or walk slowly when you let your puppy and your older dog meet, and try not to interfere.
- When you get home, if you have a garden, let the dogs meet there again in the same way before going inside. Let your puppy into the house first, before letting the older dog in.
- Lift any pre-existing dog toys and food bowls off the floor for a few days.
- If you are worried about your puppy's safety, use a baby gate or stair gate to separate the dogs in the short term, or put the puppy in his crate or a pen while the dogs get used to each other.
- Make sure all members of the family give the older dog more attention than usual.

Multiple dogs

If you already have more than one other dog, the process is the same, but you should introduce the puppy to one dog at a time.

Cats

When your puppy is this young, he is unlikely to be a problem for your cat. Besides, Labradors generally get on well with the family cat, especially if they have grown up with it. But, to be on the safe side, care should always be taken when he meets any other small pets or animals.

- Keep him on a lead when they first meet, and have a lovely puppy treat at the ready. If your cat responds by hissing and spitting to begin with, your puppy will most likely retreat. But if the cat runs away, be ready to distract the puppy with the treat so he doesn't give chase.

- Always restrain him around the cat until he learns the cat is not something to be chased.
- Distract him with a toy or a game to teach him that playing with people is more fun than chasing the cat. Okay so it's debatable, but that's what we want him to think.
- If you need to keep your puppy and the cat separated while you are out, use the puppy pen or a stair gate.
- Make sure the cat has safe places high up that it can reach instead of having to run away.

Long-term safety

Try to keep jumping on and off beds and up and down stairs to a minimum, especially if your puppy is allowed on the furniture and/or upstairs. This is much easier said than done, but until he has stopped growing, jumping can put unnecessary pressure on his hips and elbows.

11. DANGER ALERT!

Non-edibles

Your puppy will be chewing everything now, it's what puppies do best – either because they are teething or because they are using their mouths to find out about the world around them. But there are some non-edibles it's particularly important to keep out of reach:

- Medication – human medication is the biggest cause of pet poisoning
- Anti-freeze and other chemicals – many of these are sweet-tasting
- Paint thinner
- Toothpaste
- Sponges
- Pesticides
- Household cleaners (including toilet cleaners)
- A surprisingly high number of household and garden plants can be poisonous when eaten in large amounts. (See the shortlist and advice in 'Preparing for the big day'.)

- Small metal objects like coins, and nuts and bolts
- Pins, needles and other sharp objects.

Edibles that are poisonous for dogs

It's always best to feed your puppy or dog proper puppy or dog food, and simply stay clear of treats from your own plate. But there are some foods that you must never let him get hold of never mind feed to him because, while they are perfectly safe for human consumption, they are potentially fatal to dogs. These include:
- Chocolate (especially dark chocolate)
- Xylitol (artificial sweetener, commonly used in sweets and gum, but also in some sweet foods like low-calorie cake)
- Alcohol
- Onion
- Garlic
- Grapes or raisins
- Avocado

Also keep dogs away from

- Soft or cooked bones (especially from chicken or pork, as they can get stuck in your dog's throat)
- Macadamia nuts
- Fruit pips or seeds
- Potato peels or green potatoes
- Rhubarb leaves
- Baker's yeast or yeast dough
- Caffeine
- Mushrooms
- Persimmons
- Hops (generally in beer)

This is just a shortlist of some of the more common non-edibles and household foods you should keep away from your dog. It's not absolute, so it's worth keeping an eye out for fuller and newly published lists.

Swimming pools and deep water

Another clear danger is deep water. Labs might be water babies and good swimmers, but never leave your puppy by a pool or any deep water unsupervised until you are sure he knows how to swim, and is more than able, to get out.

If you have a pool, it's important to teach him where the shallowest step or exit is and how to get there. The best way to do this is to lift him into this part of the pool with you and show him how to jump out. Gradually he can learn to get back to the step (or exit point) from further away.

Some owners invest in a dog life jacket and teach their puppies how to swim right away, but unless there is real danger of falling in, it would be wise to wait until he is at least three to six months old (keeping him under strict supervision when near the pool).

Tying up

Absolutely not. Please don't ever tie your puppy out in the garden or yard. It's unthinkable that if you're reading this book you would consider this an option, but it's still worth mentioning that tying a dog up in the yard would make him frustrated, deeply unhappy and even neurotic. Sanity aside, it would put him at risk of hurting his neck or choking; prevent him from escaping from unpredictable danger, such as other dogs, fire or flooding; or simply from seeking shelter from fearful situations like loud bangs, or thunder and lightning.

12. THE FIRST WEEK

From just three weeks old your puppy has been socialising and learning to play almost exclusively with his mother and litter mates. Now suddenly he must learn to be with you, and with your family and friends. This means he has to figure out a whole new set of rules. Luckily for you he is at his most impressionable during these early days, so the time and effort you put in now to building a positive relationship will be worth buckets of good behaviour over the months and years to come.

Mesmerisingly cute as he is, your gorgeous bundle of innocence needs to know his position in the household. He needs to understand straight away that you are the leader, and a strong one at that, or there will come a time when he will be walking all over you and making the decisions.

We will look at discipline and obedience training later but for the moment, if he does something you don't want him to do, don't punish him or show aggression in any form. That would only confuse him and make him fearful of you.

Instead, distract him and encourage him into doing something good. Then reward him when he does it. Encourage and reward him – praise him at every opportunity for the good things he does in your eyes so he can begin to learn what is right in your world.

Be clear and consistent in your praise and he will become the most doting and loyal friend you could ever imagine.

Love him unconditionally

Do this, and the rest will come naturally and easily.

Teach him his name

Use his name to get his attention, and reward him when he responds to it. But be careful not to say it over and over again or he will quickly become de-sensitised to it.

Make his special place appealing

Associations with the crate or his special place must be positive, so it should never be used for punishment. Make it comfortable and leave toys and treats inside so that it always feels welcoming and homely.

If he has soiled in it, be sure to clean it well.

Encourage him into this space and praise him when he uses it.

Feed and water him

Your puppy should be having three (or maybe four) meals a day at this stage, ideally of the same food he was having with the other puppies in the litter. If you don't know how much to feed him, work out his daily allowance from the instructions on the food packaging. Split this allowance into three of four equal portions and work out a schedule for regular feeding, for example:

- Three feeds: 7am, 12.30pm and 6pm
- Four feeds: 7am, 11am, 3pm and 7pm.

(Make sure the last meal of the day is a good two hours before bedtime so that he's less likely to mess in the house during the night.)

If he's on dry puppy food, you can add a little warm water and let it soak for a few minutes before feeding him. This makes it easier to eat and digest.

And if you have more than one dog, feeding them separately will prevent any possible food aggression.

Water should always be available. If it runs out he'll start looking for alternatives and you don't want him heading for the toilet bowl. Labs can be great training for owners who don't keep the lid down.

And the water should be fresh. Don't cheat by just topping it up. Empty the bowl, scrub it clean and refill it every day.

REMINDER

Never let him get hold of anything listed in the previous chapter: 'Danger alert!'

Manage toilet time

Remember that your puppy needs regular toilet breaks and that it's up to you to help him with the when and where.

During the day, take him outside every hour if you can, and lead him to the spot you'd most like him to use. When he does it there, make sure he understands that was a good thing by making a HUGE fuss of him. Give him a treat and tell him what a brilliant, amazing, spectacular dog he is.

At night, he won't want to go to the toilet in his special place but when he is very little he can only hold on for so long, so ideally you should be getting up during the night to take him out, as well as early each morning.

"But what about when he does mess inside?" you ask. What of it? He's a baby. Clean up well and be extremely patient. No matter what you've heard or read until now, don't punish him. He won't understand. (There's a whole chapter on toilet training coming up soon.)

Handle him

Your puppy needs to learn that he is safe with people, that they mean him no harm, and that he has no reason to fear them or react defensively.

He should start learning this straight away through lots of physical contact. Pet him and handle him: fondle his paws, move his legs, run your hand over his tail, feel his ears, touch his nose, gently examine his teeth, rub his tummy, groom him, bath him, pick him up and carry him around.

Play with him

Spend lots of time playing with him. And even now – when he should stay inside your property until his vaccinations have taken effect – you should encourage him to experience the world through different surfaces. Put him on floor tiles, wood, carpet, grass, sand, rock, soft cushions, paper and blankets. Let him get used to them all.

Give him quiet time

He needs some time on his own too so he can learn not to be anxious later on when you aren't there or able to play with him. (See 'Time alone' in the next chapter.) Shut him in his special place for an hour, once or twice a day. If you have a garden or back yard, let him outside without you, or just with your other dogs, for ten minutes every now and then.

Loosen his collar

Check the fit of his collar every few days. He is growing fast and it'll need to be loosened regularly. Remember that you should be able to fit two fingers between the collar and his neck.

Insurance

If you're planning on taking out pet insurance, but haven't got round to it yet, do that now.

Visit the vet

Regulations vary from country to country, but take his vaccination certificate with you and your vet will advise you on what your puppy needs and when. Most vaccines require several rounds, between six weeks and 16 weeks, so scheme these in during this first visit.

Be sure to tell the vet if you have plans to take your puppy to puppy classes or boarding kennels, because either of these require further inoculation.

Get advice on deworming, and the prevention of parasites.

If your puppy has not already been microchipped, it's advisable to have that done now too.

If your puppy's baby nails are very long and catching on everything, you could ask the vet or a veterinary nurse to clip them for you, or to show you how to do it yourself.

Make the visit fun for your puppy by giving him praise and attention, staying by his side when he gets his shots, and telling him how good he is. Possibly take him for a walk or give him a treat afterwards to create a positive association.

13. EIGHT TO ELEVEN WEEKS

FRAGILE! HANDLE WITH CARE

Your puppy is weaning himself from his mother and you need to be ultra-sensitive to his feelings. Of course, you should always be sensitive to his feelings, but this is the worst time for anything to frighten him! From eight to approximately eleven or twelve weeks is the strongest bonding period with your puppy, so it's especially important that you give him lots of time and patience. But this is also known as the 'fear period'. It is a stage when puppies are over-sensitive and when negative stimuli are the most likely to leave a lasting impression. For example, a loud electric storm when your pup is all alone could lead to a lifelong fear of storms.

But this is also a time of opportunity. If he's already afraid of something, it's a good time to try to recondition him. For example, if he's afraid of umbrellas, show him that you are not afraid of them. Handle them gently in his presence without pressuring him in any way.

And from eight to eleven weeks is a particularly good time to show your puppy that most experiences are harmless. The more you expose him to the real world now, the more confidence he will have going forward.

SOCIALISATION

The best way to help your
puppy adjust to his new life in
your world is to socialise him
when he is still young. You
will be able to teach him fancy
dog tricks for years, but these
next few weeks are the most
important for getting him out and
about. Use them well and don't
let them slip by.

Socialising means introducing him to as many people and animals of all shapes, colours and sizes as possible. Visit friends and have friends to visit him. If puppy parties and puppy training are on offer in your area, take him along. (The chapter 'Stepping out' looks at how to do this safely and considerately.)

HABITUATION

He should also be exposed to as many new places and conditions as possible. In all fairness, you can't shut him indoors then expect him to behave normally around new people, places and things.

Take him with you everywhere you can and let him explore. Let him discover different smells, surfaces, sounds and sights. Take him into a park, to the school gates, for a walk along a river. Go to a sports match, go to the shops, paddle through puddles. Walk him over and under bridges. Let him see cars and trucks and trains and planes. Thunder, lightning and snow might be hard to arrange, but ideally let him experience different weather conditions too. Take him out at night and in the rain.

Feeling safe

It is imperative though that during these new experiences he feels safe as well as having fun. Helping him to feel at ease in new situations will go a long way towards helping him grow up to be a happy and well-adjusted dog, so stay with him through these new discoveries and don't let any of them frighten or over-excite him. Going forward, he can only be properly receptive to your training when he is feeling confident and secure.

Here are some ideas to help with this.

- If you come across a potentially frightening situation – some big kids playing rough and tumble at the park for example – watch him closely for signs of discomfort. If he is hiding between your legs, or tucking his tail between his legs, you should back off and find a different route.
- Never put him under pressure to get close to anyone or anything.
- Be alert and sensitive to his feelings, so you will know when you can approach and when to stay away. There are many signs which mean different things in different contexts. (See the chapter 'Puppy-People Translator').

- If you are not sure how he feels, avoid having a tight lead, so he knows he has a choice. If he is curious, approach from a distance. Let him look, listen and smell, gradually closing the distance as he is comfortable.
- You might want to pick him up and let him watch from your arms, but always be there for him as a reassuring presence.

Accidental noise

Don't forget about background noises that you are accustomed to but might well frighten your puppy.

TV and radio – Be especially alert during this time to sounds on TV or the radio. Dogs barking aggressively in a chase involving hounds, for example, could leave him terrified. Turn the sound down or off if he becomes alarmed – and before then if possible.

Tension in the house – Keep a good vibe in the house. If he hears angry voices or senses a bad mood, he won't understand that it has nothing to do with him (whether it does or not).

Fireworks and thunder – Close doors and windows, and muffle the sound with your own music or voices. Stay close to your puppy, showing him that you are not afraid.

BARKING

It's especially important not to punish barking between eight and eleven weeks of age for all the reasons we've mentioned. Your puppy should be allowed to explore and to express himself.

If he is barking because he is worried about something, and you know that fear is unfounded, lead him away from it and give him a treat. Reassure him with a gentle voice, then gradually expose him to whatever it is that he is afraid of, showing him that you are with him, that you are not afraid and that there is nothing to worry about.

AGGRESSION

As breeds go, Labradors have very low levels of aggression, but don't let this lull you into a false sense of security because any dog can develop aggressive behaviour. An excellent way to prevent this is by handling your puppy lots and often while he is very young. Teach him now that you can hold and touch him, his toys and his food whenever and however you please.

How?

By doing just that. Handle him, his toys and his food whenever and however you please. (Refer to the section on handling in the previous chapter.) That way he is less likely to become territorial and possessive over what he considers to be his things.

There is always a reason for aggression, and it is usually founded on fear and insecurity. But whatever the cause, it is unacceptable towards you and others.

SMALL CHILDREN

It is widely accepted that having a dog as a cherished member of the family is good for children's emotional development. But small children need to be taught how to behave around your puppy, and they must be supervised when they play with him.

Put yourself in your puppy's paws and imagine small children rolling around on the ground with you, giggling and shrieking, and how quickly that would encourage you to mouth and nip. Imagine being picked up continually, carried around, possibly even dropped, pestered, woken up. Think what it would be like not to be able to say, 'I don't want to play any more'. The only way your puppy or dog knows to tell someone they're hurting, tired, frightened or have had enough is to growl or snap. And the best way for you to manage this is to not make your puppy have to deal with it from the start.

The following points are reiterated from the chapter 'The homecoming' where we first talk about the importance of teaching small children that your puppy is NOT a toy.

- They should not be allowed to pick him up.
- They should not be allowed to disturb him if he is sleeping or has taken himself to a quiet place.
- They should not run around squealing, and if the puppy becomes over-excited they should be calm and still.
- They should be allowed to play calm games, but nothing involving wrestling or tugging.
- They should stay on their feet while playing, because if they writhe on the ground with the puppy, the puppy is likely to treat them like his litter mates and mouth and bite.

FURTHER CRATE TRAINING

If you are using a crate and it started off at your bedside overnight, you should move it further from the bedroom – step by step if you like – to its permanent day-time position in the house. But only do this as your puppy grows in confidence and don't rush it. Your job is to build his trust.

If your puppy is going to be in the crate for a lengthy period while you are out, then you should leave him with some food as well as his water and toys.

FEEDING

When?

If your puppy was on four feeds a day with the breeder, then by ten to twelve weeks you should be cutting this back to three times a day. Divide his daily food allowance (according to the instructions on the pack) into three portions instead of four and alter your schedule for regular feeding to, for example, 7am, 12.30pm and 6pm. And remember to avoid feeding too close to your bedtime, so he's less likely to mess in the house or his crate during the night.

Change of food

If you are changing your puppy's food, incorporate the new brand slowly. For example, for two to three days give him one quarter of the daily allowance of the new food with three quarters of the daily allowance of the old. A few days later make it half of one with half of the other, again for a few days, then increase the new food to three quarters and finally the full meal.

It's common for dogs to be hugely enthusiastic about a particular food the first few times they try it and then suddenly change their minds. Don't buy more than one bag of a new food at a time so that if he's lost interest in it by the end of the bag you can soon let him try another brand. Mealtimes will always be high-points in his day, so it's only right that you should shop around for a food he loves.

There's a baffling array of dog food brands and flavours on the market, so if you're making this decision without the advice of the breeder or your vet, don't skimp – with dog food you generally get what you pay for. Make sure you choose a high-quality food that is appropriate for his age. This is because puppies and adolescents need higher levels of both protein and fat in their diets than adult dogs.

Although dogs prefer meat-based to plant-based foods, a balanced meal is one that combines both. That said, many Labradors do not get on with a diet with a high percentage of grain. If your puppy is letting off excessive gas or displaying signs of an allergy, you could try moving him to a low-grain or grain-free food.

You can supplement his diet with carefully chosen chews and treats, but avoid feeding him scraps from the table because, weight aside, this leads to begging and drooling.

REMINDERS

- *Don't let him con you into giving him more food than his daily allowance.*
- *If he gulps his food down, don't give him rawhide treats. Although pet shops do sell them for dogs, they are not ideal for fast eaters (including most Labradors).*
- *Don't let him get hold of anything listed in the chapter 'Danger alert!'*

TIME ALONE

Dog owners are increasingly aware of their dogs' need to be socialised and exposed to everything, and many go to great lengths to arrange this exposure. But just as many owners forget that being alone is one of these experiences. In fact giving your puppy time alone is giving him one of his most essential life skills.

Labradors are social and don't like being alone, but most of them **have** to be alone at some time or another and the best way to minimise or even prevent separation anxiety at a later stage is to start leaving your puppy on his own now, just occasionally, during the day. If he is lucky enough to be right by your side for most of the time this is even more important. As with all his training, start practising this slowly.

- Choose a time when he is getting tired and likely to sleep soon.

- Take him outside for a little play and a toilet break.
- Shut him in his crate or special place with everything he needs.
- Ignore any whining and leave the room or go out for a short while.
- If he is very little and goes to sleep while you are out, open the crate door when you return so he can get out when he wakes.
- Start off with about ten minutes and build it up slowly to no more than an hour at this stage. For one thing, he will be needing the toilet.

COLLAR

Check daily that his collar is not getting too tight. He is growing fast and it'll need to be loosened regularly. Remember, you should be able to insert two fingers between the collar and his neck.

GROOMING

Brushing

All Labradors shed, whether they're Black, Chocolate or Yellow, so it can't be avoided or minimised by choosing a certain colour. Some Labs, very considerately, shed in bursts, and when these dogs are not shedding they truly don't need much grooming. But many Labs just shed all year round. So if there's a part of your house you want to keep fur free, the only real way to achieve this is to keep that area totally off limits.

But there's lots of good news too:
- You can cut down on the shedding with regular brushing – 'regular' being anything from daily to

at least once a week. When your puppy is grown up and in a high-shedding phase, grooming once a day or even twice daily will make a massive difference to the volume of hair in your house.

- If/when your dog is not shedding, one grooming session a week is usually enough – unless he's been rolling in something unpleasant.
- There's no real need for the grooming parlour.
- Your dog will love being groomed and what's more brushing strengthens the bond between you.
- It also keeps his skin healthy and helps you to pick up on any lumps, sores or parasites.
- And it is very good for teaching him to be handled, which is especially important during vet visits.

To help your puppy get used to grooming, start with a brush with soft bristles, and have very short sessions in case he's getting restless. It's quite normal for him to want to mouth the brush at first, so be patient with him. He will soon learn to enjoy this time with you.

When he is older and his coat is thicker you can also use a stiffer brush with fine, bent wires, as these are better for shedding the soft undercoat.

Washing

Because your puppy's natural oils are keeping his skin and his coat healthy, you should avoid bathing him too often. (Even when he is older he shouldn't need more than four or five baths a year.) He does need to learn about baths while he is little though – and it's so much easier to handle a Lab puppy than his eighty-pound adult self.

Indoor baths

- Use your own bath or a washtub. If you're using the bath, place a non-slip mat on the bottom.
- It's also advisable to put a strainer over the plug hole to prevent his hair from clogging up the drain.
- Use a quality dog shampoo, have towels at the ready, and wear old clothes and a good sense of humour because you **will** get wet.
- Ease him into the bath or washtub, offering lots of praise and treats.
- Run luke-warm water over him (ideally with a hand-held sprayer) before soaking him with a wet sponge.
- Rub in the shampoo and lather, then rinse several times, working the shampoo out with your hands.
- Bathe his head last because this is when he will shake the most. And avoid spraying water in his ears.
- Wrap him in a towel before he shakes too much and rub him down thoroughly.
- If you want to accelerate his drying, you could try getting him used to a hair dryer. Start a little at a time and blow in the direction of his coat. And NEVER use a dryer on a hot setting – always cool or slightly warm, and tested on yourself first.
- When his coat is almost, but not completely, dry is an excellent time to give him a good brush because a lot of hair will be loose from the wash.

Outdoor washes

On hot summer's days you might prefer to wash him outside. You will need a hosepipe and a clean surface that won't get muddy. You will most likely also need a helper to hold him for you. Either that or a space where he can't run off.

TIPS

Dilute the shampoo with water. This will make it go further and make it easier to work into a lather.

Holding a hand over the base of one ear will prevent him from shaking all over you. But step right back when you let go.

Nails

Whenever your puppy's nails get unmanageably long they will need clipping. You might well have had them done at his first vet visit, but eventually they will need clipping as often as every month or two, so it will pay off in the long run to buy your own clippers now and learn to do it yourself.

Labs are not especially keen on having their paws held, so the sooner your puppy gets used to having his nails clipped the better. This is obviously not something you can practise every day, but what you can do to help him get used to the idea is to choose a time when he is already relaxed, then take hold of his paw and tap his nails gently with the clippers. When he responds calmly, praise him or give him a treat.

The next stage is to hold his paw and clasp a nail in the clippers – without making the clip but still showering him with praise when he stays calm.

When you are ready to make the cut, hold the nail so you can clearly see it from the side. You want to avoid the 'quick', which is inside the nail and contains sensitive nerve endings, so clip a tiny bit at a time, inspecting after each clip to make sure there is no bleeding. If you have a Yellow Lab, look for the part of the nail you can see through if you hold a light to his paw.

If necessary, do no more than one or two nails at a time, praising him after each session, then making a note of the ones you've done. Eventually your puppy will be comfortable with the process. If you want, you can file the nails smooth with an emery board.

Teeth

There are lots of treats on the market that double as dental chews to clean your puppy's teeth and keep his gums healthy. If you want to clean his teeth and to clean them by brushing, you can buy dog toothbrushes and meat-flavoured pastes.

EXERCISE

All dogs need exercise so they don't get bored, unruly, overweight or unhealthy, and your full-grown Labrador will need an hour to two hours of exercise a day. But between eight and eleven weeks of age take your puppy on two to three walks a day of no more than 10-15 minutes at a time. As a rough guide, add five minutes to the length of each walk per month, so that by four months, he should ideally have walks of approximately 20 minutes each. As a rule, more shorter walks are better for puppies than fewer longer ones.

The chapter 'Stepping out' is full of advice and tips for your outings.

TRAINING

This isn't a now-and-then exercise reserved for obedience classes. It's an ongoing, moment-by-moment

process that starts the minute your puppy enters your life. Training is about mutual understanding, clear communication and a better life for your puppy as well as everyone else in the family. This means that every member of the family and household should be involved, using the same set of rules, spoken commands and body language.

The chapters 'Behaviour' and 'Training' cover the key DOs and DON'Ts to help you build a strong foundation for a relationship based on understanding and respect.

PLAYTIME

This doesn't mean putting your puppy outside with his toys. Play is social interaction. So you, or a member of the family, needs to actually play with him. In fact playtime is so important that there's a full chapter devoted to this too, with key pointers to help you make every game and every play session a positive experience. The chapter also has ideas for toys and games, and it won't take long for you to figure out his favourites as well as the games you play best together.

NOTE
Puppies grow up fast compared with human children. One week in your puppy's life is equivalent to around five months' development in a human child.

14. TWELVE WEEKS PLUS

Although at twelve weeks your puppy is still heavily dependent on you and ever so eager to please, he will start leaving your side to explore more. You will still be on his radar all the time, but you will begin to stop tripping over him whenever you step backwards.

His socialisation is still incredibly important and should be ongoing. As for chewing, he will be munching on everything.

Teething

By twelve weeks, your puppy's adult teeth, a full 42 of them, are waiting to push out those super-sharp baby teeth. It then takes until around 18 weeks for those baby teeth to even start falling out. That's a lot of weeks of important chewing to be done so – for the sake of your puppy, your house and your sanity – keep valuables out of reach, and always have an abundant and ready supply of toys and treats that he is allowed to chew on.

We will look at chewing again under 'Discipline'.

TIP
Tie a knot in an old cloth, wet it and
put it in the freezer. Then give it to him
when it is frozen to ease his sore gums

Sleep

By this age, your puppy no longer needs the 18-22 hours' sleep he needed when you brought him home, but he does still need a good 16 hours of rest or sleep a day.

Food

Twelve weeks to five months: For now, keep to three feeds a day. And remember not to feed him too close to your bedtime.

Five months to a year: By five months you can gradually bring the meals down to twice a day, which is how often he will need feeding as an adult dog, although some owners do cut this back to just one feed.

If your puppy is not faring well on commercially produced food, you could try putting him on a raw diet, which is home prepared food with an emphasis on raw meat, whole or crushed bones, vegetables, fruits, raw eggs and some diary. There is a lot of controversy around the subject of raw diets, so if you are considering this route, you will need to research the subject thoroughly.

Overfeeding: It is important not to let your Labrador get overweight at any stage of his life. These dogs are sporting and are meant to be healthy, strong and fit. Research into Labrador health in relation to weight shows that keeping your dog lean vastly reduces the risk of numerous diseases, and can extend his life by up to two years.

The following chapters (right up to 'Puppy-People Translator') focus on the most important and pressing puppy issues in terms of behaviour and training, and are filled with tips to help you as you guide your little one into adolescence and beyond.

15. BEHAVIOUR

Your puppy loves you so much! He wants to learn from you and please you. But he only knows what his survival instincts tell him, so, to reiterate, it's your job to teach him what is and isn't allowed in your world. We will look at specific behaviours in the next chapters, but the pointers in this general chapter are fundamental to all of these.

For a well-behaved puppy, the first thing to understand – as you surely do by now – is that puppies are much more receptive when they have nothing to fear. A fearful puppy will never be totally engaged.

Our understanding of animal behaviour is improving all the time, and it's no longer acceptable to punish dogs, never mind puppies, by shouting, smacking and rubbing their noses in the carpet. This sort of treatment is both ineffective and counterproductive. It scares your puppy and puts you in a bad mood. You lose your dog's trust and the spinout of that – into all the other areas of the relationship – is just not worth thinking about. You want your puppy to be happy and optimistic, looking forward to everything, rather than fearing it.

So how do you achieve this? In a nutshell: you gain his trust by focusing on the things he does right. By encouraging good behaviour and rewarding it!

Encourage and reward

Always tell him what you DO want him to do, rather than what you DON'T want him to do. Let's say for example he's got the TV remote between his teeth. Don't shout and get angry! Calmly distract him with something else, something he IS allowed to chew on. Refocus him on this new and exciting toy, and rescue the remote. If you don't have anything at hand, then ask him to do something to obey you – even something as simple as a 'Sit!'

His feelings are everything

Let's say your puppy bounds up to you with a glint in his eye, a wag in his tail and a captured, dishevelled bathmat in his mouth. Try not to think about your favourite bathmat which, after all, is just a thing and has no feelings at all! Instead, think about HOW HE'S FEELING about what he's done. He thinks he's done brilliantly, doesn't he? He wants a medal. Scold him now and you'll really confuse him. Then again, if you praise him, he might keep bringing you bathmat-type presents ad infinitum. So what do you do?

You don't scold or praise. Distract him instead by calling him to you and getting his attention onto something else, a toy perhaps. When he is refocused on the toy, offer him a tempting chew. By then the bathmat should be far from his mind, and you should be able to rescue it. And if it's still functional, remember to hang it up out of his puppy-jaw reach for a few months.

You are the leader

To establish a positive relationship, your puppy must understand from the start that, even though you love him and you are best friends, your word is law and he must listen to you. And he will, as long as you are a worthy leader and a good teacher.

Here are some key tips for you.

- Don't be aggressive towards him. Instead, be gentle but firm.
- Don't go too easy on him either. In the long run that can be as unfair as punishing him.
- Be crystal clear in your instructions. Use single words rather than sentences and try to be consistent in your choice of words. Don't switch between 'Come!' and 'Here!' for example, or 'Off!' and 'Leave!'.
- Keep your tone positive.
- Use body language as well as verbal commands.
- When he does what you want, show him unreservedly how clever he is. Be happy and excited and reward him with praise.

Timing is all-important

It's vital that you teach your puppy with timely signals – signals that apply to what he is doing AT THAT TIME. If you discipline him for something he did two minutes ago, he won't understand the reason. For example, if he runs off after a cat and then comes back, and you shout at him for chasing the cat as he is coming back, he will naturally think you are shouting at him for coming back and not for chasing the cat. The result? He is confused and intimidated, and next time he will think twice about coming back.

Too many well-meaning dog owners make the mistake of misplaced timing – and it's simply unfair.

Rules must be consistent

We've been here before, but this is really important. If one person lets your puppy onto the sofa, it's downright unfair for someone else to reprimand him for being there. Rules will be very confusing if they differ from person to person, so it's really crucial that everyone in your puppy's life understands and teaches what is and what isn't allowed in precisely the same way.

Prevent bad behaviour

- Try to anticipate things that might go wrong. If you think he's about to chase the cat, hold on to him and distract him with a toy. Dangling tablecloths, for example, are begging for trouble. Don't use them until he's older.

- Make sure his basic needs are met: love, food, water, warmth, things to chew on, sleep, play, exercise and exploration. If he has all of these he is far less likely to behave badly in the first place.
- Don't put temptation in his way. If you don't want him eating from your dinner plate, don't leave it lying around, unattended and in easy reach. That would just be setting him up to fail.

Let him know when you disapprove

In many bad behaviours, the best way to tell your puppy you don't like what he's doing is to take away something he wants – your attention. Discourage bad behaviour by ignoring him when he is behaving in any way that is not acceptable to you. Stop play, walk away, look away, leave the room if you can.

When to say 'No!' or 'Leave!'

1. When your puppy does something totally unacceptable, something that could endanger his life for example.
2. When he boldly ignores your voice command because he would rather do something else.

These need to be corrected immediately and here's how.

- Reprimand him straight away. Say 'NO!' or 'LEAVE!' in a voice that is loud and startling enough to prevent or stop his behaviour. It should be in stark contrast to your usual quiet and calm voice, and used sparingly for best effect.
- Block his way with your body, or physically stop him if you need to.
- Then make eye contact and use your voice to get him to focus on you.

- Once you have his attention, praise him for changing his focus.
- The flaw with 'No' and 'Leave' is that your puppy doesn't know what he's meant to do instead. Always try to give him something better to do or to chew on.

Still struggling?

If you've tried all these things with a bad behaviour, with repeated, clear and consistent communication, and you're still struggling, you can resort to time-out. Shut him in the kitchen, or a similar and safe place, and leave him for a few minutes – five is acceptable, ten is too long.

Alternatively, and as a very last resort, you could restrain him in a safe and suitable time-out spot and ignore him for no more than five minutes. The lead should be just long enough for him to be able to sit up and lie down comfortably. (But **never** go out and leave him like that.)

Serious behavioural problems

Yes, even Labradors can develop serious issues. These include constantly demand attention, jumping up on people, chewing on everything, behaving in a destructive manner, barking incessantly, nipping, biting, growling, showing aggression towards other dogs, and even relieving themselves inside the house. But all of these problems are caused by something, be it boredom, loneliness, lack of socialisation, lack of training, fear, anxiety or insecurity, being spoilt or badly treated, or even just poor breeding.

With behavioural problems, it is especially important that you are able to tell the difference between playfulness and aggression. See the chapter 'Puppy-People Translator' for clues on reading the signs. If your puppy develops any traits that could endanger you, himself, or any other person or their dog, you should get help from a professional in dog behaviour. And the same goes for any other serious behavioural problem.

Let's look at the most common issues in some detail.

16. JUMPING UP

Your Labradorable puppy will jump up because he is happy to see you, because he loves you, because he wants to lick you all over your face and he can't reach, because he wants you to pet him and play with him. Although he is used to jumping up on his mother and litter mates, he now needs to learn not to jump up on you or other people. You might not mind his jumping up right now – after all he is not likely to bowl anyone over with his loving greetings while he is such a little tyke – but when he is a big, heavy adult he could easily send someone flying.

And size aside, don't forget about those muddy paws and sharp claws. Basically, jumping up soon becomes a nuisance and you want to nip it in the bud before it gets out of hand. So:

Don't
- Reward him for jumping up
- Talk to him
- Tell him to get down
- Push him away
- Shout or yell
- Smack him or use physical punishment of any sort.

Do
- Step back so that his paws don't reach you
- Look away from him
- Turn away from him
- Lift your hands away and don't touch him
- After a few seconds, come back to him, and repeat if necessary

- When he has quietened down and stopped jumping, be sure to praise him and reward him.
- Get all family members to do this, and ask regular visitors to help with this too.
- If jumping up on visitors is likely, put him on a lead before opening the door to them.

How does it work?

These methods will eventually teach him that if he jumps up he will get no attention, and that if he keeps his four paws on the ground he will be praised.

17. TOILET TRAINING

Remember, at first your puppy has no idea that the house is not a public toilet. This is something you need to teach him – and with time and patience.

In a nutshell, initially you will need to take him outside hourly and show him where to go. When he does go in an acceptable place, and as soon as he has finished his business, it's time to celebrate. Reward! Reward! Reward! That way you will teach him that doing his business outside means AMAZING things will happen.

Here are some key DOs and DON'Ts to help speed up the process.

Do

- When your puppy arrives at your house for the first time, give him a guided tour. The sooner he understands that all this space is living area, the sooner he will stop using it as a toilet.
- Take him outside every hour.
- Also take him outside immediately if you spot any of these tell-tale signs:
  ○ Sniffing and circling the floor
  ○ Whining
  ○ Pacing up and down
  ○ Scratching the floor.

- Lead him to the spot you'd like to encourage him to use.
- Then wait. And wait some more. Stay out there with him – come rain or shine – watching him all the time.
- You can spur him on with an encouraging command, like 'quickly now' or 'wee time'.
- Wait until he's completely finished before you reward him, or he might only do half his business.
- As soon as he is finished, shower him with praise.
- When he goes to the toilet inside, thoroughly clean the place he's marked and use a pet-safe odour eliminator. Your puppy is most likely to go to the toilet somewhere he can already smell wee or poop, so the best way is to teach him where to make his messes is to keep your house clean. (If possible, limit your puppy's access to carpeted areas.)
- If he has messed inside but on a training mat or piece of newspaper, carry this outside to where you'd like him to go in future, and weigh it down there with something heavy so it can't blow away. The smell will act as a signal to him to do his business there.

Don't

- Punish him for piddling or pooping inside. Punishing him for something he can't help and doesn't fully understand would only make him nervous and slow his progress.
- Leave him outside on his own. He will just turn his attention to getting back to you, and when he does get back inside the house, he will very likely still need to go.

How long will toilet training take?

Labradors are renowned for being easy to housetrain. Progress obviously varies from puppy to puppy, but it's safe to assume he will leave the odd surprise for you until he's around six months of age, and it could take up to a year for him to be accident free. Be patient.

NOTES

- *Your puppy will never wee or poop to spite you.*
- *Some dogs make a little wee as a sign of submission, and some wee with excitement. These are mere lapses and should never be punished!*

TIP

Once your puppy understands that you want him to do his toiletries outside, you can hang a bell on a string from the door that leads to outside. He might well learn to jingle the bell to tell you when he needs to go out.

18. MOUTHING AND NIPPING

All puppies love to play, and play in the litter involves mouthing one another, so it's completely natural for your puppy to want to play-bite. He might also bite because he is teething. If, like many new puppy owners, you don't mind your puppy chewing your hands now, you soon will. As he gets older, the biting will get harder and involve others too, so he should learn as soon as possible not to use his teeth on people.

Adult dogs are good at controlling the pressure of their jaws, but puppies often make the mistake of biting too hard because they are still learning and practising jaw control. If a puppy bites one of its litter mates too hard while playing, the hurt puppy will yelp and stop playing. Your puppy has already learned from the other puppies that biting too hard inhibits play time.

He will learn gradually to play more gently until he understands not to let his teeth into contact with your skin at all.

Do

- Play with him with a chew toy in your hand, encouraging him to bite the toy. If he bites you instead and inflicts pain, make a high yelping sound and immediately withdraw your hand. This is exactly what would have happened with his litter mates, so it will help him to learn that it's okay to nip the chew toy, but not your hand.

- If the biting persists, remove yourself from the game, the room even, just for a few minutes to show him that teeth on skin equals no more playing. It's not a quick fix, but he will gradually make the association.
- Supervise small children. Their tendency when a puppy mouths them is to scream and run around, which only excites and encourages the puppy even more.

Don't

- Shout at him or smack him if he mouths or nips. This can make the biting harder to control.
- Rush him. He can only learn jaw control gradually and through experience.
- Play rough tug games – they just encourage biting.

19. CHEWING HOUSE AND HOME

'Puppies are constantly inventing new ways to be bad. It's fascinating. You come into a room they've been in and see pieces of debris and try to figure out what you had that was made from wicker or what had been stuffed with fluff'

Julie Klam

All dogs chew, especially puppies! They chew things either because they are teething or simply to explore. Chewing is how they learn about the world around them – they don't have hands, so they inspect everything they can with their mouths and teeth.

Your puppy will chew on anything he can, so it's really important to give him things you are happy for him to chew on.

Don't

- Leave valuable and tempting chewables, like shoes, lying around on the floor. Labradors were bred to carry things in their mouths so anything left lying around is fair game. (Puppies are excellent training for untidy owners.)
- Don't leave supposedly-less-tempting chewables lying around either. With a Labrador this includes the likes of spectacles, sunglasses, mobile phones and even car keys.
- Encourage sticks. They can splinter and get stuck in his mouth.
- Buy him rawhide chews. If eaten too fast, they can get stuck in his throat.
- If you find your puppy chewing something he shouldn't have, don't try to take it away from him. He might decide to swallow it.
- And don't start a tug-of-war.

Do

- Instead of trying to pull or coax a forbidden item from your puppy, replace it with something he is allowed to chew on – and make sure this replacement offering is something you know he loves. As he plays with the forbidden item, hold the new and better offering to his nose and say, 'Leave!', 'Drop!' or 'Off!' – whichever of the command words you have chosen to stick to.

- When he drops it, you can give him the treat and a pat.
- Make sure you have lots of puppy toys and treats. (Pet toys are created to appeal to your dog by smell, taste, feel and shape, but you can also use old soft toys.)
- Keep these prizes close by. You never know when you'll be needing them.
- If you see your puppy approaching something with demolition on his mind, call him with a happy voice. Puppies are easily distracted, and he should immediately forget what he'd planned to do and come running to you. Reward him for coming and give him something more suitable to get his teeth into.
- If your puppy's got a taste for something that can't be moved – a table leg for example, spray it with a pet-friendly anti-chew, or citronella.

TIP
Don't give him old socks, slippers or shoes.
It might give him the idea that all your
footwear is there for the taking.

When will it end?

Your puppy's need to gnaw on everything in sight will go away, but it won't happen overnight. In fact, it will probably take well over a year.

20. DIGGING

It's absolutely natural for Labradors to dig. That's not to say your puppy will, because not all Labs do. But if your puppy does take too much of a liking to digging, here's something you can try.

- Find him a place where he IS allowed to dig.
- Bury things for him in that spot and let him find them.
- Then, if you find him digging in other places, tell him 'No!' or 'Leave!', refill the hole he has made, and show him again where he can and should dig instead.

SOMETHING TO TRY

If the problem persists, make an unpleasant clanging noise whenever you see him starting to dig. Hit a pot with a metal spoon for example. Soon he'll associate digging – either in that place or altogether – with this horrible noise.

21. BARKING

Many Labs "don't bark enough" according to their owners, but just as many bark "too much". If your puppy is a barker, he will bark for very good reason, no reason at all, just for fun, to make suggestions … and sometimes even to make demands. Yes, he will have a whole box-full of bark tricks, each with their own distinct message. You will soon learn the difference between barks that are attention-seeking and those that are genuinely nervous or excited.

Barking at others

It's natural for him to warn you about strangers or intruders, and that kind of barking is not necessarily something you want to stop or even discourage. Let him bark at them, just momentarily, then call him back to you and praise him, or distract him with a toy or an exercise if you need to.

But if your puppy is barking at a passer by – or the neighbour's cat, which is more likely at this stage – and you do want him to stop, your instinct is probably to shout at him to keep quiet. But put yourself in his shoes and you will see that if you shout at him while he is barking, he is likely to interpret your shouting as 'people barking', and think you are egging him on, or even coming to help. The result? He will bark even harder.

So with unwanted barking, as with pretty much all bad behaviour, it's more effective to give him the 'I'm ignoring you now!' treatment.

- Don't talk to him or touch him
- Instead turn away from him
- Leave the room or area if you can
- If he won't stop barking and it's becoming a problem, you could distract him with a loud noise (like hitting a pot with a metal spoon)
- When he has settled down and come to you, you can acknowledge and reward him for his new-found quiet behaviour.

Barking at you

As your puppy comes to see that his efforts to win your attention, like jumping up or nipping, are fruitless, he might well replace these with his latest greatest trick – a demanding bark that says:

- I am still here
- Stop ignoring me
- Hey, I want some of that too
- Come on, let's play.

Whatever it is, he wants your attention. Don't give it to him. Instead, pull out your now-well-practised ignoring techniques:

- Look away and turn away
- Don't talk to him
- Lift your hands away and don't touch him
- Leave the room if you can.

But, as always, when he has quietened down, be sure to acknowledge and reward him.

Incessant barking

This is seldom without reason, and the reason is all too often because he is lonely, frustrated, bored or needs attention. For example, if he is left on his own for long periods, shut in a small space or, worse still, tied up, he WILL bark incessantly. And who could blame him? Even a mature Labrador would do that. In cases like this, where the barking is linked to a genuine need, it is the cause that needs to change.

Do

- Move him to a less isolated place.
- Arrange for there to be more space for him to play in.
- Take him for long or longer walks.
- Give him more time to interact with you and other dogs.
- Get another dog. Being left at home alone all day is hard on any dog, but Labradors really are sociable animals. They need company and one of the simplest solutions would be to get another dog.

Don't

- NEVER leave your puppy alone for a long time, never mind in a small space. It's simply not fair.

22. STEPPING OUT

Once your puppy has been fully vaccinated you can
start walking him out and taking him on outings. But
first he needs to practise walking on the lead at home
and while you're waiting for his vaccinations to take
effect is the ideal time.

Eventually you want him walking by your side on
a loose lead, but for a puppy, with seemingly endless
stores of pent-up energy, this is surprisingly difficult to
learn.

Do

- Use a normal collar (no choke chains) and a six-foot non-extendable lead.
- Attach the lead when he is calm and not resisting you.
- Start by letting him wander around the house with the lead trailing behind him, but try not to let him chew it.
- The next stage is to pick up the lead and encourage him to walk along beside you.
- If he pulls, stand still and call him to you. Praise him, then try again.
- When he is walking nicely alongside you, with the lead slack but off the ground, reward him generously with praise and treats.

Don't

- Use a choke chain or half check.
- Drag him. That would only make him panic and pull away.
- Be pulled along by him. That would teach him that pulling works in his favour.
- If he is pulling, don't pull back, or yank on the lead, or shout at him. Instead, stop and call him to you and praise him for coming when he does.

When the time comes for him to get out and about, here are a few things to consider and be aware of.

Safety

Think carefully about where you're going to take him so you can avoid frightening or stressful experiences.

- Choose a safe, open space away from busy roads.

- Choose a place where other dog owners are likely to act in a responsible way.
- And think about the best time to go. Perhaps it's too soon for a Saturday morning at the park if there is likely to be a noisy sports match in play.

If something does scare him on an outing, let him know you are with him, protecting him, and that he is safe.

What to take:

Make sure you have him on his lead (a short one is better to start with) and arm yourself with:
- Biodegradable poo(p) bags – more than one
- Treats (ideally in a treat pouch) – so you can reward good behaviour
- Water and a bowl – if there is no clean water where you are going. (As a space saver, you might like to invest in a pets' water bottle with a flap or lid that doubles as a bowl.)

Pooping

If he poops, pick it up with a poo(p) bag and dispose of it at home (or in a public dog waste bin if one is provided).

Other dogs

When you come across other dogs on your outings, you could use the opportunity for your puppy to practise his meeting and greeting. But never assume that other people or their dogs are happy to reciprocate. And never let your dog run up to other dogs unless their walkers have told you it's okay. There are lots of reasons why it might not be. Perhaps the dog is very old; maybe it is injured; in recovery; not good with puppies; or the owner is working on a specific training exercise. Always ask first and from a distance:

1. whether their dog is good with puppies and
2. whether they are happy for your puppy to say 'hello'.

If it is okay for your dogs to meet, stay close by to supervise, and to pre-empt any bad experiences.

- Make sure you walk on past some dogs, and people too, so your puppy doesn't take it for granted that he can run up to anyone for a chin- and tail-wag.

Play dates

If your puppy meets another dog he plays especially well with, you could arrange play dates at times that suit you both.

Together time

- Put your smart phone out of temptation's way and make this quality time with your puppy!
- If you are going somewhere with big open spaces like the park, you can take a long, extendable lead. But NEVER pull your puppy back with the line. He should come to you as called. There is more on this in 'Training'.

23. EXERCISE

Labradors are bred to be fit and athletic. As an adult, your dog will want to run and play till you drop – yes, **you** – and then some! So unless you're a bit of an athlete yourself, it'll be up to you to find ways to give him the exercise he needs.

Walking

Walking is fantastic, low-impact exercise for you both. Once your puppy is walking nicely on the lead, you can start picking up the pace, gradually working up to a brisker walk and over longer distances.

When he's fully grown, he'll need walking several miles a day – half a mile at the very least – and if you want to head for the hills, adult Labs make great hiking partners.

Running

Never jog with your puppy because his bones are still forming, but adult Labs make fabulous running partners too. If you decide to start running with him when he is fully-grown then, as with the walking, you would need to work up the distances slowly.

You would also need to be mindful of his paws. Dogs aren't well booted like you, so stay away from long stretches of hard ground and be aware of surfaces that might be very hot, or cold and icy.

Swimming

Labradors are powerful swimmers, with webbed paws set between long toes, and 'otter' tails that steer like rudders. Most of them take to the water like ducks.

But if yours is hesitant, start him somewhere with a gradual incline into the water and go in with him. He might try to walk on the water at first, lifting his front feet right out with each step. If he does this, hold his bottom up so that his front feet stay underwater.

If he walks in, then stops before he loses contact with the bottom, you could support him under his ribcage, keeping him level until he gets the hang of it. But don't push him into anything he doesn't want to do.

In the long term, swimming is fantastic exercise for a Lab – low impact and easy on the joints.

Games and playtime

These also count towards his daily exercise and are especially fantastic for mental stimulation. The chapter 'Playtime' is filled with ideas and tips.

BUT

All of these activities come with their own risks – some obvious and others totally unpredictable, so here is a shortlist of things to be alert to. The list is not meant to have you deprive your puppy or dog of the great outdoors and the exercise he absolutely must have; it's just to help you avoid taking chances with his safety.

On land:

- Even if your puppy or dog is hugely reliable off the lead, blind trust is still careless. Don't let him loose anywhere near traffic – he can cover a lot of ground very quickly and squirrels, rabbits and deer for example could lure him on a merry chase.
- Make sure you know the area well before letting him off the lead – apart from roadways, be aware of cliffs, drainage culverts and thin ice.
- Although your dog might feel invincible on a walk, some animals will get the better of him. As far as possible, keep him away from porcupines, skunks and snakes.
- Be careful not to let him graze on greenery on hikes. Not all tasty plants are agreeable, or even safe.
- If he's walking along the coast, keep him away from dead fish.

In water:

As a basic rule, if he is swimming take the same precautions with him as you would with a young child.

- Very cold water can cause hypothermia, which could drain him of his strength to swim to land.
- In the sea, stay clear of rough waves, undertows and side currents.
- Rivers are dangerous when they are fast-flowing, eddying or moving towards a waterfall or weir.
- Be especially careful of steep banks – natural drops as well as manmade ones on the edges of ditches and canals. Anything he could not easily get out of.
- If it's a swimming pool he's in, make sure he knows where the step is and how to get out.
- In the wild, consider the possibility of other animals in the water: alligators, crocs, sharks, snapping turtles.

24. TRAINING

'Properly trained,
a man can be dog's
best friend'
Corey Ford

You most likely assume that puppy training is about training your puppy – most people do – but in actual fact it is nearly all about you, the owner, learning how to communicate effectively with your puppy.

And puppy training is not about tricks either. To reiterate, it is about basic obedience to improve communication and understanding. Why? For a better quality of life for you, your puppy ... and everyone he meets.

Everything from the chapter on Behaviour applies to this chapter too because the premise for training is the same. Because your puppy is more engaged when he has nothing to fear, you should train by encouraging and rewarding good behaviour. Always tell him what you DO want him to do, rather than what you DON'T want him to do.

And training should be fun. The best trained dogs wag their tails during training because they enjoy the challenge as well as the reward.

Reward-based training

Praise is always a motivator in training, but it is often not enough, and it is now commonly accepted that training with food-motivation, at least at first, has the best results. Initially, then, praise is a secondary reinforcer. In time, you can wean your dog from the food-based training, and he will obey you purely for the fun of the training itself. But even then, you should reward him with treats intermittently.

When to start

Training starts the moment you bring your puppy home. Even if you've signed up for puppy classes at some future date, don't wait. Teach him what you can, little by little, moment by moment. Practice often, and never give up. (It's worth mentioning here that while it is never too early to start training your Labrador, it is also never too late.)

Who's responsible

Anyone and everyone in your puppy's close and extended family – and all using the same spoken commands, hand signals and body language.

Where?

Start training in a quiet place with no outside distractions. A closed room is infinitely better than a park with other puppies play-fighting nearby.

What?

By the time he is six months old, your puppy should know his name and obey your orders to: 'Come', 'Sit' and 'Down'. He should also have been introduced to 'Stay'.

How?

All commands should be spoken clearly, firmly and with confidence. At least initially, lengthen the vowel sounds and make sure the consonants are crisp and clear.

Your voice and treats are key to training your puppy, but don't forget about gestures. It might surprise you to learn that most dogs actually respond better to body language than to words.

Name Recognition

One of the first things your puppy needs to learn is to recognise his name. After all, how else will he know that you're communicating with him?

Do

- From a short distance – three or four feet is fine – call your puppy clearly, using his name just once.
- Use a happy, friendly voice.
- Crouch down if you can.
- Open your arms to welcome him (body language is hugely important).
- Make a fuss of him when he gets to you.
- If he doesn't respond, wait a few seconds then call again, still clearly, and still just the once.
- When he does come, praise him lovingly, give him a small treat and tell him how brilliantly clever he is.
- Practise this often.

Don't

- Overuse his name or say it repeatedly in quick succession, or he will soon learn to ignore it.

EYE CONTACT

If your puppy is not looking at you, he is probably not listening either. Calling his name will encourage him to look at you and, when he does, you can know he's engaged. He's turning to you to find out what's coming next: will you open the door, take him for a walk, throw the ball? It's excellent that he's turning to you for answers and provision, so make sure you reward him.

CALLING HIM TO YOU

If your dog only knows one command it should be 'Come' or 'Here'. Coming to you when he's called is important for your relationship, and essential for his safety too. Recall is much like the name recognition exercise and now, while he is little, is a very good time to teach it to him because this is when he needs you more than ever for love, food and safety. In fact, if he's already joined your family, chances are he is with you right now, under your feet or helping you to absorb this book. Digest it even. And chances are he already relates the recall command to something fun and exciting: food, a new toy or play time.

Do

- Follow the steps in the Name Recognition exercise above, using his name and adding a calling word like 'Come' or 'Here'. Consistency is key, so choose which word you prefer and stick with it.
- Call him to you often, gradually increasing the initial distance between you.
- Practice at home and on a lead before you let him go when you are out and about.

- When you do let him off the lead away from home, make sure it is in a very safe place. Then practise letting him go and calling him back.
- If he keeps following you anyway, find someone who can help you by holding him while you back away. Then entice him, if necessary, and when he is struggling to get to you, your helper can let him go. Only then, when he is running to you, call his name and 'Come' or 'Here'.
- Your welcoming body language can be very helpful with this too. Try getting down on your haunches or your knees and opening your arms to greet him.

Don't

- If you call your dog to you and he gets side-tracked en route, you might be tempted to scold him when he finally arrives. But coming to you should ALWAYS be associated with good things, so never punish him if he doesn't come straight away. If you do, he'll associate the scolding with the last thing he's done – come to you. Then, understandably from his point of view, he'll think twice the next time about coming back at all. (See 'Timing is all-important' in the chapter on Behaviour.)
- Don't always put him back on a lead when he comes to you, or he will soon learn that coming means the end of his free-play session. Only put him back on the lead after several recalls.

TIP
*If he develops the habit of running up to you
but then dancing around just out of your reach,
start withholding his treat until AFTER
you have a grip on his collar.*

132

'SIT'

This is one of the most useful exercises you can teach your puppy.

- Call him to you and hold a treat, palm facing down, just in front of his nose for him to smell.
- When you've got his interest, slowly take the treat up a couple of inches and over his head (slightly behind and above his eyes).
- When he lowers his bottom, say 'Sit!' and give him the treat.
- Once he is doing this well, you can move on to the next stage. Wait until his bottom is actually on the floor before you say 'Sit!', and only then give him the treat.
- He will soon learn to associate the word with the action. In time you can teach him to sit for longer stretches, from further away and during distractions.

NOTE
Be careful not to ask him to 'Sit down!' if you only want him to 'Sit!', because once he has learned the 'Down!' command as well, he won't know whether you're asking for a 'Sit' or a 'Down'

'DOWN'

- It is best to start teaching this command when your puppy is already in an attentive sit.
- Without feeding him the treat in your hand, move your hand, still palm down, from above his nose and towards the floor, between his front paws and close to his body.
- When he lowers his nose and front paws, keeping his bottom on the ground, say 'Down!' in a clear voice and give him the treat.
- When he is doing this well, you can wait until his tummy and all four paws are flat on the floor before you say 'Down!', and only then give him the treat.

NOTE
You need to be careful with this command too – not to use it when he is on a piece of furniture he is not meant to be on. If you shout 'Down!' at him to get down off the sofa and he is already 'lying down', you will just confuse him. Rather say 'Off!'

'STAY'

This is an essential command for the safety or your puppy – or any dog that would otherwise dash out the front door, across a road, or leap out of the car.

The training involves teaching him to remain in a Sit or Down position for increasingly long times before you reward him.

- Once he is in a 'Sit' or a 'Down', say 'Stay!' in a strong but soothing voice, and combine this with a clear hand signal. With your arm straight, your palm flat and your fingers together, point to the ground just in front of him.

- If he gets up, simply ask for the Sit or Down position again and repeat the 'Stay' command.
- When he has stayed for a few seconds, say 'Good!' (or another 'release' word of your choice) and give him a treat.
- Gradually work up to longer times, but no more than 30 seconds, and step back in increments to increase the distance. (There's no point giving him unrealistic goals, so the idea is to push him to the limit while letting him succeed.)
- Keep him on a lead when you put this command into practice at the front door or in the car.

What if the training's 'not working'?

If your puppy doesn't do what you've asked (assuming he's not hard of hearing):

- he doesn't understand and needs clearer instructions,
- he needs more practice,
- or he needs a better reason to obey you – like a treat, an even better treat, or higher praise.

EXPANDING ON THE BASICS

Extension exercises

Duration – Once your puppy can do an exercise, like 'Sit' for example, you can gradually ask him to sit for longer periods before treating him.

Distractions – You can slowly increase the distractions too. A 'Sit' when a squirrel is taunting your puppy from a nearby tree is very different from a 'Sit' in a quiet place. Once he's mastered the instruction in a quiet room, start practising it in a busier part of the house, then at the park, then on a street corner, and so on.

Distance – In time, you can also begin asking your puppy to 'Sit' from slightly further away from you, but start with just a couple of steps and don't forget the all-important hand signals.

Advanced commands – If you'd like to add to these basic commands, your puppy can go on to learn 'Stand', 'Settle', 'Heel' and many more. There are some excellent obedience training books on the market, and if training classes are available in your area, they are well worth the effort and your dog would absolutely love you for taking him.

25. PLAYTIME!

Playing with your puppy helps to develop his socialising, improve his communication skills, and give him the mental and physical exercise Labradors so badly need. Most importantly of all, it's great fun. But whether you're just messing around or trying something more structured, you should always keep these Rules of Play top of mind.

- Start playtimes when your puppy's being good, so you're not rewarding him for bad behaviour.
- Several short play sessions spread throughout the day are always better than one long one.
- Whatever games you're playing, remember he's only little, so don't overpower him. Be sure to match your strength, speed and energy to his own.
- As far as possible, get down low to his level (small children excepted).
- If a toy is involved, avoid hard tugging. Never let his feet leave the ground as he clings to a toy. It puts too much pressure on his teeth, and encourages more aggressive play. Holding the toy by your fingertips is a good way to manage the pressure.
- When your puppy wins the toy, encourage him back to teach him that playing is more about having fun together than possession.
- If the playing does shift from fun interaction to possession of a toy, then stop for a while.

- Always try to calm the playing down before you stop. It's disappointing stopping a game when it's at its most exciting.
- And always end playtime on a good note. If you've had to stop for a moment, restart the game and end it when things are quiet and friendly.

For playtime to be great fun, you just need each other – there's no need for fancy toys or expensive equipment. Sharing a walk, throwing a ball and paddling in the shallows can be the most special times. But if you're still looking to expand your activities and further enrich your time together, here are some ideas.

GAMES

All puppies have their favourites and you will soon figure out which ones you play best together.

Chase

This game is excellent practice for encouraging your puppy to come to you when he is older.

1. Flick a treat across the floor.
2. Let him chase after it.
3. When he comes back for more, make eye contact and praise him.
4. Only then flick another treat across the floor, and so on.

Fetch

This is an extension of Chase, but outside or in a much bigger space.

1. Throw things for him to fetch: toys, a ball, a treat.
2. Say 'Fetch!' as you throw each item.
3. Once he knows to fetch, start throwing the objects into harder-to-reach places.
4. If this doesn't work, throw more interesting toys or tastier treats.

Catch

You can play this with toys, treats and balls.

1. Start with something light and easy to grab hold of, like a floppy soft toy.
2. Throw it in an arc over his head, so that if he stayed in place it would land close to his muzzle.

3. If he misses, try to pick it up before him and he will soon learn that if he wants it he must catch it before it hits the ground.

4. When he's learned to catch, you can move on to balls as well. (Much later he can progress to frisbees which are even more challenging, but be sure to start with a soft disc.)

Which hand?

1. With your hands behind your back, put a small treat or two in one hand and nothing in the other.

2. Make your hands into fists and bring them in front of you.

3. Let your puppy choose which fist he prefers the smell of.

4. When he's decided which hand he's interested in, and it's the right one, say 'Good!' and open your hand, letting him take the treat.

Treasure hunt

Your puppy will love this! Labradors excel at sniffing things out and relish any opportunity to put their skill to the test. What's more, rooting around for hidden treasure can be played just as well indoors as out.

1. The first time you play, let him follow you and watch as you hide a treat (something he can eat), then lead him away and say 'Find'.

2. As a next step, you could ask someone to hold him while he watches you hide the treat. When you get back to him, you can let him 'Find'.

3. Once he understands how the game works, you can make sure he can't see you at all when you hide the

treat or a toy. Then lead him into the room or area of the garden where it's hidden, say 'Find', and this time he will have to follow your smell. (The first few times you might need to guide him.)

One day, when he is older, well trained and fully understands the game, you can make it more difficult by using 'Sit!' and 'Stay!' while you hide the treat, and then by hiding it in more difficult places too.

The memory game

When your puppy is a little older and has mastered some easy games, you can move on to more difficult challenges, like this one.

1. Put a treat in a sealed box or bag (because we want him to remember where it is rather than sniffing it out) and let him watch while you hide it.

2. Lead him away and distract him (for no more than 30 seconds at first).

3. Then say 'Where is it?', and initially you might need to guide him.

4. When he understands how the game works, you can make the distraction time longer and longer.

Obstacle course

1. Turn your passageway or garden into an obstacle course – build jumps, make tunnels, fill a tea tray with water, arrange boxes to navigate around … anything you can think of that is safe.

2. Guide your puppy through the course and reward him with treats each time he overcomes an obstacle.

TOYS

To keep your puppy interested in his toys, don't put them all out at the same time. Only let him play with or chew a few at a time, and rotate them during the day or through the week.

Presumably he'll have a range of toys that roll, bounce or squeak – toys that are wonderfully chewy or simply soft and cuddly. But here are three ideas for playtime that are a little more interesting and challenging.

The maze

There are a number of 'slow feeder' pet toys on the market which are maze-like in design. They are intended for dogs who gulp their food down too fast, but they also work brilliantly for brain-training.

- Put a treat or two in the middle and let him use his paws, snout and tongue to work the treats out of the maze before he can eat them.

The hollow chew

Hollow toys made of hard rubber, the Kong for example, are available online and from most pet stores. Fill one of these with small dog treats, or even with peanut butter (as long as it contains no Xylitol), or marmite if you can get hold of it. Your dog will spend hours trying to crunch or lick out whatever you've filled it up with.

Activity balls

There are plenty of these on the market in a range of shapes and sizes. Put dry food or treats inside one of these and your puppy will love rolling it around to get the pieces out.

EQUIPMENT

Use your imagination, but make sure whatever you come up with is safe, and well secured where necessary.

- Hay bales can be used as jumps, steps and passageways
- Old tires make fabulous jump hoops
- Children's paddling pools are great fun for playing in as well as cooling off in on hot days
- Look in children's toy stores – tunnels, playhouses and sand boxes will appeal to your puppy too.

26. TRAVELLING BY CAR

Of course your puppy would love nothing more than to stand on the front passenger seat, stick his head out the window and feel the wind in his face, but car travel is not the time for free play.

Ideally you should invest in one of the following, depending on whether you want your dog to travel on the back seats, or – if your car has a rear door – in the space behind the back seats.

- a seatbelt harness – well-padded and comfortable, that fastens securely into your vehicle's existing seatbelt fitting,
- a crate or cage that is small enough to fit in the back area of your car while also being big enough for your adult dog to sit up and have a stretch in,
- a dog guard – fitted between the back seats of your car and the trunk/boot area.

All of these are available in pet stores and online.

Never

- Get him into or out of the car on the traffic side of the road.
- Allow your puppy or dog on your lap while you're driving.
- Allow him on the front passenger seat, especially if an airbag is fitted.

- Tie him in place on the back seat by his collar and lead instead of using a proper seatbelt harness.
- Leave him strapped into the car in the blaring sunlight. This would hurt him just as much as it would you.
- Leave him unattended in a hot or even warm car for more than five minutes. Dog fatalities from heatstroke in cars are frighteningly common.

Do

- Whenever you are getting your dog into the car or letting him out, make sure it is on the pavement side of the road.
- For everyone's safety, use a doggy seatbelt, crate or cage, or dog guard.
- For his own safety, teach him to 'Stay!' in the car until he is given the command to exit.
- On long journeys, stop regularly to let him relieve himself and stretch his legs. These stops will also help ease any car sickness he might experience.

27. PUPPY-PEOPLE TRANSLATOR

Your dog understands your every word, or so it's said. The point is, your choice of words is very important. Even more important though is how you say them. Be clear in your body language and be gentle but firm, patient, loving, encouraging, reassuring.

It is also said that a dog can say more with his tail in just a few seconds than his owner can say in hours. If he's already in your life, you will be familiar with his favourite expressions: 'I am so happy to see you!' and 'You are the best thing that ever happened to me!'. In his earliest days with you, you will no doubt have braced yourself for, 'Your face is like a lovely lolly!' And before long – but only if you've been 'good' – you could be surprised by another frequent favourite: 'Your training is coming along very nicely!'.

Yup, a lot of your puppy's body language is really easy to read, but truth be told the signs are not always straightforward. How good are you really at understanding his language? By way of example, a wagging tail can be a sign of happiness as well as one of aggression, so we need to look at the whole picture including: how he wags it, what the rest of his body is doing at the time and what else is going on around him. To help with this, here are some Puppy-People translations:

I love you — Racing to meet you
- Wagging tail
- Licking
- Whimpering

**I'm happy
and excited** — Tail wagging fast (but watch out as this can also be a sign of concentration or aggression)
- Racing around
- Whimpering
- Pulling lips back and exposing teeth

Let's play — Wagging tail vigorously
- Rolling head
- Dashing off and jumping back again
- Jumping in front of you, facing you, front legs splayed out
- Elbows on the ground and bottom in the air (the play-bow)
- Bounding leaps
- Running in circles
- Lying down or rolling over
- Barking intermingled with growls (can be confused with aggression)

What is that I
hear? Where is it
coming from?
- One paw raised
- Head tilted to the side
- Brow raised
- Ears twitch and nose wiggles
- Mouth may be open and panting

Totally
chilled out
- Lying on back with legs flopped out
- Curled in a ball
- Lying down watching you

Feeling
submissive
- Rolling over onto back, exposing
  tummy and genitals
- Tail between legs
- Head dipped or tucked in, ears
  pinned back

I'm curious, and
maybe a little
concerned, about
something going
on out there
- Raised paw

I'm frightened
or unhappy
- Tail between legs
- Cowering, or lying down
- Ears twitching back and forth
- Staring ahead at object of fear
- Lying down with paws ahead,
  looking ahead, ready to run

- Raised hackles (hairs along the top of his back)
- Whining
- Whimpering
- Looking to you for help

I'm in pain or frightened and want your help

- Looking from you to whatever it is he needs, and then quickly back again
- Whining or whimpering
  This is not manipulation. It's a genuine plea for help. Tell him you're there for him and he can count on you.

Aggressive

- Standing up straight
- Ears pinned back, or sharply forward
- Raised hackles
- Low growl with eyes fixed in a direct stare
- Body is tense, ready to attack
- Tail held stiffly, or wagging in stiff, quick, stilted movements
- Barking
- Sudden unpredictable bites
- Growling or biting (as a response to punishment or in defence of food or toys)

I'm warning you   - Snarling
                      - Growling
                      - Baring fangs

**Feeling lonely
and locating
other dogs, or
sending out
a warning**   - Howling
                     - Baying

**I want your
attention: 'hello',
'look at me',
'I'm bored'**   - Barking directly at you

**I'm begging
you. Pleeez!**   - Whining, with pleading eyes
                     *Yes, it's a heart-wrenching expression,
                     but don't give in to that cute little face.
                     Your environment will help you to tell
                     the difference between manipulative
                     begging and 'I'm in pain or frightened
                     and need your help'. If you're eating a
                     juicy steak that he's hoping you'll share,
                     it's safe to assume he's begging.*

28. GOING FORWARD

Somewhere between six and 18 months your puppy
will go through adolescence, and this is usually the
most difficult period for owners. He is growing in
independence; his chewing continues relentlessly; and
he will become more territorial. Hopefully the solid
foundations you've laid in the early weeks and months
will make this stage a little less wearing. Remind
yourself it is short-lived.

Your puppy is also beginning to show the onset of
sexual maturity and is likely to go off exploring
because she or he wants to mate. Females will come
into season around the nine month mark (usually
between six and twelve months) and be overcome with
the urge to roam, and males will begin mounting
things, marking their territory and maybe even
fighting with other male dogs. Both sexes will
experience hormonal changes that are likely to affect
their behaviour, so if you're not planning on breeding,
having your dog neutered (castrated or spayed) can
make all the difference.

Neutering

To neuter or not to neuter? This highly controversial
subject is beyond the parameters of this book. Suffice it
to say that most vets and breeders consider neutering
the more responsible option.

But the best age for neutering is also open to debate. This is because it varies not just from breed to breed but also from dog to dog. Ideally it is when your puppy/dog has reached physical as well as emotional maturity, so the best timing is all about getting the balance right between the two. Physically, the average Labrador will reach its full frame size and adult height between 12 and 18 months but it can continue filling out and gaining muscle until it is two. Emotional maturity is more difficult to pinpoint, but less bounce and reduced chewing are both good indicators.

Early neutering in Labs has been linked to health as well as behavioural problems, and it is commonly agreed that, while waiting might cause some inconvenience to the owner in the short term, you shouldn't have your puppy neutered until after a year. The average view of the responsible breeders I have consulted puts 14 months as a safe and sensible age.

Running off

If your adolescent puppy starts running off – most likely because he wants to mate – and this behaviour persists, prevention is always the better option. At home you will need to keep him inside or in a fully-enclosed garden or yard, and while walking out he will need to stay on the lead.

But if he does run off (or away), be sure to praise him when he comes back (or home). Never scold him when he gets to you, because in coming back he is being a good puppy. That way he will want to stay with you (or home) and, even if he does run off again, he will always want to return.

Fear period

As if adolescence isn't tricky enough, between seven and eight months of age your puppy could also experience another fear period, so you do need to be especially gentle and understanding around then.

The special place

When your puppy is toilet trained and has stopped
eating everything in sight, you will be able to start
leaving the door to his crate or special space open. In the
meantime, remember to keep praising him when you see
him going in there on his own.

Feeding

Because Labradors have little in the way of self control
when it comes to food, it is your job to manage your
puppy's food intake and keep a check on his weight.
Extra weight puts unnecessary strain on his joints and
organs, so if you do notice that his weight is creeping up,
immediately cut back on the treats. Between five months
and a year old you will also be able to cut his feeds back
from three times to twice a day.

At around a year you can move him on from puppy
to adult food. And remember that if he shows signs of a
food allergy – by scratching, licking or chewing his legs
or paws, or rubbing his face – switching to a low-grain
or grain-free diet could help to alleviate the symptoms. If
his food bowls are plastic, switching to stainless steel or
ceramic has also been said to make a difference.

Nails

Apart from being uncomfortable, nails that are too long
can cause splayed feet and lameness. Some very active
Labs never need their nails clipped, but most do. You
can tell that your dog's nails need a trim:
- if his toes splay apart,
- if his nails scratch the ground when he's standing
  upright,
- or if you can hear them clacking on the floor.

Not all Labs have dewclaws – the nails higher up on the insides of the legs – but if yours does, these will need trimming too to prevent them from catching on things or growing into the skin. Some owners used to have their dog's dewclaws surgically removed, but nowadays, unless they are malformed or causing discomfort, the practice is avoided.

Fine tuning

This book sets out to answer the most important early-stage questions on owning a Labrador puppy. It covers the things you need to know when he is still very young – the things you don't want to get wrong in his vital first months.

At a later stage you might well choose to fine-tune your training, or need to deal with specific behavioural issues that might've arisen. There are some excellent and extremely thorough books on the market. And if you've got the time and inclination for obedience training classes, they are incredibly enriching for both you and your dog. He would love you for taking him, forever and more.

29. STANDOUT LABRADORS

ENDAL

It seems fitting that the most decorated dog in the world should be a Labrador. Endal's awards included 'Dog of the Millennium' and the PDSA's 'Gold Medal for Animal Gallantry and Devotion to Duty'. Working for a disabled ex-Royal Navy Officer in the 1990s, Endal was the first dog known to place an unconscious human being in the recovery position without training. He was the first dog known to use a 'chip and pin' ATM card, and the first to ride on the London Eye. He managed a remarkable range of day-to-day chores including loading the washing machine and picking items from supermarket shelves.

ZANJEER

Countless people owe their lives to Zanjeer, a detection dog who spotted weapons and ammunition used in serial explosions in Mumbai in 1993. This Lab helped detect 57 country-made bombs, 175 petrol bombs, 11 military bombs, 242 grenades and 600 detonators. He was most known for his contribution to the police force for detecting 3,329kg of explosive chemicals.

JAKE

Abandoned as a puppy, with a broken leg and dislocated hip, this Lab grew up to become one of fewer than 200 US government-certified rescue dogs. He became a national canine hero after the 2001 September 11 attacks, when he burrowed through 'white-hot, smoking debris' in search of survivors. He also helped search for Hurricane Katrina victims in 2005.

DAISY

This Lab saved the life of her owner, Dr Claire Guest, when she warned her about her breast cancer. (Claire is now founder and chief executive of the UK charity Medical Detection Dogs.) Daisy passed on in 2018, having sniffed over 6,500 samples and detected over 550 cases of cancer. In 2014, this extraordinary dog was awarded the Blue Cross Medal for her pioneering work.

LUCKY AND FLO

These twin Black Labradors, trained as counterfeit detection dogs, became famous in 2007 for sniffing out nearly two million unlicensed counterfeit DVDs for the Motion Picture Association of America while on a secondment to Malaysia. The pair later repeated a similar feat in stores across New York.

SABI

This Australian special forces explosives detection dog went missing in action in Afghanistan. It was almost 14 months before he was recovered safe and well in 2009.

SALTY

Omar Riviera was on an upper floor of the Twin Towers at the time of the 2001 attacks. Despite extreme confusion, noise and panic, his yellow Labrador guide dog Salty led him down 70 stories just before Tower 1 collapsed. Omar tried to release Salty so he would have a better chance of survival, and a co-worker tried to lead him away, but Salty refused to leave Omar's side.

FICTION AND ADVERTISING

The fictional Labrador, Marley, from John Grogan's best-seller *Marley & Me* has become a household name. Another popular Labrador figure is the Andrex puppy mascot, featured primarily in UK advertisements for Andrex toilet paper (known elsewhere as Scott or Kleenex Cottonelle).

YOURS TRULY [_____]

Because I know you have invited a standout
Labrador into your home – a puppy that is already
heroic in its own right.

30. THERE WILL BE TIMES ...

This book is intended as an easy read to offer you some shortcuts with the theory. But there are NO shortcuts with the practice. The practice needs patience and repetition, encouragement and reward.

Tough times

There will be times when your puppy does all sorts of things you don't want him to. When he's bored and teething, he will set his alligator jaws to work, chomping their happy way through your designer chairs. He will gift you with shredded items of now ex-value – and with random deposits of unidentifiable bodily waste – because with his eat-first-ask-later mentality, all manner of edible and inedible items will disappear down
the hatch.

He will slop his muddy paws across your cream-coloured carpet, then wait until he's well and truly indoors before shaking off the rest of the muck. He will bark when he has something to say, and whine when he's upset or lonely.

For months, your house will be littered with toys, and the pitter patter of determined paws will be under your feet when you go to the fridge, the toilet, the shower and the front door.

There will be many times when you're at your wits' end and you will look at him and think, 'What **have** I got myself into?'

Well it's this: you have a new family member who, when he is fully grown, will literally bowl you over with his boisterousness. He will distribute his coat generously, far and wide. If you let him, he will take up space on your bed, sofa, passage floor and/or entrance area. In fact, wherever he is allowed you will be navigating your way around him. His soft eyes will be pleading, "How long till the next meal?" With his "love everybody" attitude, he will welcome strangers to your door and then show them around. He will need so much exercise that you'll struggle to keep up. And if you aren't firm enough with the rules, your new family member will soon be ruling the house.

But it's precisely because Labs are big and furry, welcoming, eager to please and bursting with energy that they are the most popular dogs on the planet. And it's precisely because of their big soft eyes, velvety coats and blundering capers that we love them so much. So remember that when you feel your patience running thin, and no matter how often your

Lab seems like a small child covered in fur, don't try to make him more human.

Just as he is, he will give you more love and more fun than you could ever imagine, and there will be many times when you ask yourself, 'How did I get so lucky?'.

Good times

Your family has grown by four furry feet and when you get home, your puppy's wet nose, wiggle bottom and thumping tail wait to greet you, ecstatic to see you. He will melt your heart, bring you buckets and buckets of laughs and enrich your life with his constant eagerness to please, bumbling antics and unconditional love. And never again will you have to pick food up off the floor.

There will also be plenty of times when he does the things you DO want him to do. Praise him – with attention, treats, toys ... it doesn't matter what, as long as it's something he loves.

Taking-him-for-granted times

And last, but definitely not least, there will be times when he just IS – a calm, quiet presence by your side. Those are the times when it will be easiest for you to forget or ignore him, and those are the times when it is most important of all to remind yourself, and him, just how special he is.

31. USEFUL CONTACTS

WEBSITES

American Kennel Club
www.akc.org/dog-breeds/labrador-retriever

Australian National Kennel Council
ankc.org.au/Breed/Detail/7

Company of Animals
CompanyofAnimals.co.uk

The Labrador Site
www.thelabradorsite.com

The Kennel Club (UK)
www.thekennelclub.org.uk

The Dog Training Secret
thedogtrainingsecret.com

The Labrador Retriever Kennel Club of South Africa
www.labclub.org.za

There are also many rescue, adoption and re-homing centres devoted specifically to Labradors – far too many to list here, but a quick search should bring up the options in your area.

INDEX